Raising Rhia

Raising Rhia

A Mother's Fight for a Joyful Life

Terena Scott

SWP

SHE WRITES PRESS

Published in 2026 by
She Writes Press, an imprint of The Stable Book Group

32 Court Street, Suite 2109
Brooklyn, NY 11201
https://shewritespress.com
Library of Congress Control Number: 2025918830
ISBN: 979-8-89636-076-6
eISBN: 979-8-89636-077-3

Interior Designer: Andrea Reider

Printed in the United States

Names and identifying characteristics have been changed to protect the privacy of certain individuals.

For Rhia

And for every parent asking, "What do I do now?" when they learn their child has a disability.

Dreams

1

My daughter's life is not a tragedy. Nor is she one of the labels the doctors gave her as she grew up. Ataxia. Optic Nerve Hypoplasia. Failure to Thrive. Mitochondrial Disease. Deaf-Blind. Hypotonia. Cerebellar Atrophy. Sensorineural Hearing Loss. Sleep Apnea. Developmental Delay. These labels describe what she has, but they don't describe who she is.

My daughter is strong, intelligent, creative, and funny. She is all these things in her own unique way. Her smile makes everything right with the world. Her eyes are dark blue when she's happy and turn to a pale glacial blue when she's tired. Her dark hair, pale skin, and ruby red lips remind everyone of Snow White in the Disney movie. Rhia takes no nonsense from anyone and fights with surprising strength despite her small limbs and weak muscles. She looks at you like she can see everything about you, inside and out, even though the world is actually one big blur to her. She is magic. She is not just a list of labels that equal disabilities.

It took me a long time to understand that.

2

RHIA'S DAD IS A POET. WE MET IN A CAFE ON HAIGHT Street in San Francisco in 1991, back when artists and freaks could still afford to live in the City by the Bay. I was studying theater at San Francisco State University while waiting tables. He was a San Francisco native who actually knew how to use a sword and shoot an arrow from a bow. We both liked to write in the same cafe, the Horseshoe, so called because of the teeth-grinding cowboy coffee that probably could make a horseshoe stand up in a bucket.

I was writing in my journal, completely engrossed in documenting the stress I felt about auditioning for the spring musical at SF State, when suddenly a piece of folded paper landed on the page I was writing on. I looked up to see a man with long black hair, dressed in a black leather jacket and tight black leggings, walking away from my table. Annoyed, I unfolded the paper and instead of seeing a phone number and a weak pickup line, there was a poem written in black ink. The poem wasn't about how I looked or anything suggestive, it was simply an observation about the intensity of my writing, which made him curious about me. It was signed, "Robin Hood."

Looking up, I met his beautiful blue eyes across the room and smiled. He took that as an invitation to join me at my table. When he sat down, I said, "Robin Hood?"

He grinned. "Only on Haight Street. My name is Laurent."

We talked for an hour before I had to go to work two blocks up Haight. I told him I'd be free at ten o'clock that night.

He met me at the restaurant as I was closing up, then drove us out to Ocean Beach, where we drank wine in the foggy darkness.

He was an excellent kisser.

I've always been a sucker for romance, and Rhia's dad fulfilled every drop of romantic longing I carried from adolescence. He was also extremely smart, which pulled me in even more. Ever the sapiosexual, I just needed him to talk to me about the Pythagorean theorem to make me weak at the knees. I was twenty-five years old, he was twenty-eight, and we were instantly in love.

Every summer he worked at the Northern California Renaissance Faire in Novato, teaching drunk "visitors" how to use a bow and arrow at the archery booth. We'd been dating for five months when he brought me to pre-opening rehearsals and introduced me to his friends. I got a job at the faire singing Irish songs with an acting guild. He designed and sewed my costume, a dark-green overdress that closed with pewter clasps on top of a *leine* (an Irish underdress with wide, long sleeves) made of undyed linen. He also gave me a leather belt

I wore around my waist, a pouch to carry money, and a pewter tankard for drinking. I supplied the lace-up leather shoes and wide-brimmed hat. On our breaks from performing and teaching, Laurent and I walked arm in arm around the fair, me in my Irish finery and he in a blue vest, breeches, white blouse, and large black hat. We talked to the visitors in our best Elizabethan accents when we weren't making out behind an ale stand. At night we changed out of our costumes and wandered the quiet streets of the faire with other performers, laughing, kissing, and toasting the stars with our matching pewter mugs shining in the moonlight.

When that faire season ended on Labor Day, I moved with him into a house with a spectacular view of the Oakland hills, affordable only because the neighborhood was lousy. I kept working on my theater degree, and he wrote more poetry when he wasn't working at 24 Hour Fitness.

People say you can't feel the moment your child is conceived, but I did; I felt Rhia's presence before her father and I had sex that night. It was our third year working together at the Renaissance Faire when Laurent and I, drunk on ale and love, decided it would be amazing to conceive a baby there. The moment the words were spoken, I felt the dark night shift, as if something unseen moved closer. A strong spirit followed me through the silence of the faire at night, up to our tent and into our bed.

One month later, I learned I was pregnant. I knew I was having a girl and her name would be Rhiannon.

When I first heard Stevie Nicks's song "Rhiannon" as a child, I found a book about Welsh mythology at the library called the *Mabinogion*. In the myth, Rhiannon is a Horse Goddess who traveled with three birds that sang to you during hard times. She also traveled between the worlds of life and death and delivered messages in your dreams. If you fell asleep thinking of a problem, Rhiannon came with the answer. I decided at age ten that if ever I had a daughter, I would name her for the Welsh goddess that Stevie Nicks wrote a song about. Luckily, Laurent liked the name too.

He and I married in the fall of 1994, in an old farmhouse in my hometown of Kelseyville, population 2,000. I wore an antique lace gown I could just fit into at four months pregnant. We cut our wedding cake with one of his swords.

3

I never planned to be a mom; I dreamed of being a movie star. Kids weren't part of that plan, but my body's ticking clock overpowered my plans and I got pregnant. I was in love, only twenty-seven, and very healthy. It should have been an easy pregnancy.

Most people have morning sickness, but I had all-day, every-day nausea and violent vomiting for the first six months. This was followed by a diagnosis of gestational diabetes requiring painful finger pricks several times a day to check my blood sugar. When the vomiting finally passed, I was granted one month of a blissful hormone high, belly round, breasts full, skin glowing and hair glossy from all the extra estrogen. I once told a friend, "I love being pregnant. I could do this forever!"

And then at the beginning of the seventh month, I walked into our overgrown backyard and began pulling weeds as if my life depended on it. My body filled with a restless hunger that made it impossible to sit still. I yanked dead weeds from parched ground with my bare hands, and when my arms were tired I paced the fence line like a cheetah in captivity. I was in labor but didn't realize it until the cramping in my belly made me moan.

Laurent rushed me to the hospital, where I lay flat on my back in a hospital bed, hooked up to IVs dripping magnesium into my body to stop contractions. I went from manic energy to exhaustion and complete powerlessness over my own body. Seven months' gestation was too soon for Rhiannon to be born healthy, so I cried and prayed and hoped the multitude of drugs would halt the contractions. Doctors came and went, but the contractions kept rolling through my womb, hard, then soft, twisting and releasing. Nothing stopped them. My cervix wedged open at 3 centimeters but thankfully didn't open any wider.

After five days in the hospital with no change, my own doctor, a dark-haired woman in her forties named Dr. Milkman (a perfect name for an OB!), asked me what I wanted to do.

"Do?" I didn't understand the question.

"You've been here five days. None of the medicine we're giving you is working. Your baby doesn't appear stressed, so what do you want to do?"

"I don't know. What should I do?"

She touched my arm and said, "This is your body. You can decide to stay here or go home. It's up to you."

My body? For months I had focused on my unborn child so that she would thrive in my womb. I had been sick, swollen, poked, measured, weighed, and analyzed. I had morning sickness that lasted six months and then I developed gestational diabetes. My blood pressure was too high and my legs were too swollen. Now I had prodromal labor, ongoing contractions that weren't progressing toward actual delivery. My child was fine, but my body clearly hated being pregnant.

"What happens if I go home?" I asked, desperately wanting to leave the hospital but afraid of hurting my daughter.

"We've done every intervention possible and nothing has stopped the contractions. If you go home and the medication stops, I don't think you or your baby will be at any more risk than you are in the hospital. Perhaps being back in your own bed at home will help. Or if the contractions worsen, you can come back."

"I want to go home," I whispered.

Laurent set up a bed on the futon in the living room where I spent a terrifying two months flat on my back, trying to keep Rhiannon inside of me. "Not yet, not yet . . ." I chanted, rubbing my belly while the contractions continued. I watched soap operas, read books, and begged my body not to give birth. A home health nurse came to check my blood pressure, my blood sugar, my cervix, and Rhiannon's heartbeat every other day. Thankfully Rhiannon and I remained stable. And then the magic day arrived when I could get out of bed without fear. My child was fully developed and Dr. Milkman predicted I'd give birth by the next day, if not sooner.

However, Rhiannon had her own plan. My stubborn daughter stayed inside my womb for two more weeks. Running up and down stairs, walking three miles, and pulling more weeds in my yard didn't budge her out of her safe cocoon. My womb kept contracting, but Rhiannon stayed put.

Dr. Milkman decided my body needed help getting into rhythm to give birth, so I was scheduled for induced labor by having my contractions strengthened with Pitocin.

On a foggy May morning in 1995, after three hours of intense contractions and hard pushing, Rhiannon Aviv was born. The sun broke through the fog the moment I held my six-pound four-ounce daughter against my sweaty chest. Her amazed blue eyes locked onto mine, and I knew I'd known her for a thousand years.

"Hello," I said.

The way she stared at me made me wonder if she recognized me too.

4

Rhiannon. My beautiful baby girl. She yelled her head off when the nurse bathed away the blood and mucus from being born and even louder when the doctor poked her heel for blood tests. Only ten minutes old and already being punctured with needles. Then it was my turn to bathe. My whole body shook with adrenaline as I washed away dried blood and sweat. I listened to Rhiannon's angry protests and couldn't bear the sound. My body felt hollow without her. We were finally separated physically, but as I showered away all traces of giving birth, I realized that my heart would never be my own ever again.

At last we were both clean and bundled up in blankets together. Rhiannon and I spent the night in the hospital for observation to ensure my prodromal labor and pregnancy-induced diabetes hadn't impacted our health. While she slept, I looked for signs of problems. Her skin was mottled red and white and her face squished flat at the top, but the nurse assured me that was due to the birth and would go away in a day or two. I counted her long, thin fingers on each hand, examined her ears, her nose, the long lashes almost touching the top of her cheeks as she slept. Her bones felt as fragile as a sparrow's, and a wave of fear made me tremble again. What have I done? How could I possibly keep this little girl safe?

"I'll try," I whispered.

A kind nurse entered our room and said, "Let's see if we can get your daughter to eat a little, okay?"

I wiped away tears and nodded.

"You're going to feel a bit weepy for a while. You have a lot of hormones doing wild things to your brain now."

"I don't know what to do," I said.

"That's why I'm here," she said, handing me a pillow to support my left arm. She helped me shift Rhiannon so that her head was cradled by my arm so she could reach my left breast, then how to guide my nipple to her mouth. Tiny drops of milk leaked onto Rhiannon's face, and she moved her mouth gently. I lifted her head higher and tickled her cheeks, but Rhiannon just wiggled her lips without seeking my nipple.

"It's not working," I said. Just one hour into motherhood and I was a failure. I couldn't breastfeed my child, which was supposed to be perfectly natural and easy.

"Don't worry," the nurse said. "A lot of babies have trouble at first. Give it time. She's probably worn out from the birth."

She took Rhia from my arms and laid her in the bassinet beside my bed. "You both need to rest. We'll try again in a few hours."

I lay on my side and stared at my daughter, eager to try again. The nurse returned every few hours to help me breastfeed Rhiannon, and in the morning a lactation specialist came. By morning my breasts ached and milk squirted out so fast

Rhiannon choked. She couldn't seem to coordinate sucking my nipple and then swallowing the milk. I mostly squirted it into her mouth, like she was a baby bird.

When Rhiannon and I were released from the hospital in the morning, I told the nurses we weren't ready. I couldn't feed her, therefore we should stay in the hospital until I learned how to breastfeed her properly. Everyone assured me it just took practice and Rhiannon wouldn't starve. The lactation expert would come to my house later that day, and in a few days it would all be fine.

Rhiannon's skin turned creamy white as the mottling faded, and her squished face became round. My mom stayed with us the first week, teaching Laurent and me how to change a diaper efficiently and how to bathe a slippery baby in the kitchen sink. When my mom left, the terror I felt in the hospital returned. Rhiannon and I still hadn't figured out breastfeeding, and I was convinced that without my mom's help I was a terrible mother. Everyone assured me I was doing a good job and not to worry about breastfeeding. Rhiannon was getting plenty of nutrition, or she wouldn't be gaining weight. She was thin, but she was healthy.

At two weeks old, Rhiannon's skin turned from soft white to pale yellow. She was diagnosed with jaundice caused by increased bilirubin in her blood, so at-home light therapy was prescribed. It isn't uncommon for newborn infants to get mild jaundice because their liver hasn't learned to efficiently handle the waste that builds up in the body. Bilirubin is part of the elimination process. It looks reddish-orange inside the body, which is why a baby's skin turns yellow. Rhiannon lay under special lights that help break down the bilirubin, wearing just a diaper and with her eyes covered for protection from the bright light. The secondary light she lay on top of was the exact same color as her Glo Worm doll.

After several days of home phototherapy, Rhia's jaundice worsened. Laurent and I brought her back to the hospital where she'd been born, this time to the Neonatal Intensive Care Unit. She was given a blood transfusion to flush away the bilirubin, then was placed safely inside a plastic incubator where she slept under intensive UV lights. I sat beside the incubator on a hard wooden chair, not allowed to hold her or touch her or comfort her. Needles poked her tiny arms and legs and a sleep shade covered her tiny eyes. Every four hours a nurse opened the incubator and gently handed Rhiannon to my longing arms. I tried so hard to breastfeed, but she sleepily suckled at my breast, so tired she fell back to sleep before getting enough from me. I stroked her cheek to get her to suck more, hoping to prolong the opportunity to hold her and give her all of the nutrition she desperately needed. But after a few minutes, the nurse took her away and put her back in the incubator.

I refused to leave Rhiannon all alone in the hospital, so I commandeered a chair in the corner of the closest waiting room, napping with my head balanced against the wall and the back of the chair. Laurent brought me dinner and sat with me whenever he had time off from work, and a few friends came to drag me out for fresh air, but mostly I sat and waited until I was called to feed Rhiannon again.

One night, a nurse woke me from a deep sleep. As we walked down the hallway to the NICU I heard a baby crying loudly.

The nurse smiled. "Hear that?" she asked.

"Yes," I said.

"That's your baby." She touched my arm and her smile grew warmer. "Your daughter is going to be fine. She has a strong cry. That means she has healthy lungs. Don't worry. You'll take her home soon."

Rhia's frustrated and hungry wail echoed down the hallway, proving to everyone in that hospital how strong she was. I will never forget that moment or the comfort I felt hearing my daughter yelling for me. That memory brings me comfort even today and reminds me of Rhiannon's strength through everything she's had to endure.

The nurse was right. After one more transfusion with blood from her dad, Rhia's pale yellow skin returned to a healthier, pink tone, and two days after the procedure she left the incubator and came home.

5

Laurent and I decided to bring Rhia with us to the Renaissance Faire that August. It wasn't unusual for people to bring a baby to Faire; in fact, most of our friends brought their infants and toddlers. Those children grew up performing at Faire alongside their parents, singing and dancing or just being adorable in their handmade cotton costumes, which were passed down to younger children. Rhia inherited a white cotton gown and tiny white cap once worn by a baby who was at that time eight years old and dancing with her mom. The Irish Guild, the acting troupe I still worked with, was more than just a group of performers. If you work with the same group of people year after year, share meals and costumes, watch each other's children, laugh together, and support one another through hard times, you become a family. To this day I am still close with the people I performed with under the giant oaks at Black Point Forest more than twenty years ago, even though the Faire is no longer there.

Rhia was embraced wholeheartedly by the Irish Guild, and I dreamed of how she would become a fully fledged "Faire Brat," the name for children who grew up at the Renaissance Faire. I imagined how Rhia would sit beside me and sing songs when she wasn't chasing her friends around the wishing well. That summer, people cooed and whispered over the tiny, beautiful baby girl who slept in a wicker basket at my feet. Every day I was asked by a visitor, "Is that a real baby?"

Unfortunately, Rhia hated the faire. When she wasn't sleeping, she cried. Other moms in the Irish Guild held her and walked so I could eat or run to the "privy," taking turns to try to console my miserable daughter. Laurent brought her to the archery booth for an hour each day to give me a break. At night, Rhia cried harder, and I knew her cries woke up everyone in our campsite, but no one complained, at least not to me. I felt frantic. Why wouldn't she stop crying? Other people managed to care for their baby at Faire; what was I doing wrong?

We didn't know when Rhiannon was a baby that all the noise, movement, heat, and general cacophony of the Renaissance Faire overwhelmed her delicate nervous system. She was unable to comprehend or regulate the onslaught of stimuli around her. We didn't know she had a neurologic disease and was blind.

Not every day was filled with crying and stress. There were moments when Rhiannon actually smiled, especially in the morning when the day was cool and quiet or when music was played. She particularly loved it when I sang to her or when my dear friend Tama played the Celtic harp.

On a full moon night at the end of August, the entire guild stood together in a circle at the top of a hill overlooking Faire while my dear friend Tama led the Blessing Ceremony, welcoming Rhiannon to the Irish Guild family. Each person in the guild held her for a moment and said welcome or hello, then passed her to the person standing beside them, demonstrating that each of them would be there for her throughout her life. On that night, Rhia didn't cry. She quietly looked at each person when they held her as if studying them. Sometimes she smiled, and several times she laughed.

Before Tama concluded the ceremony, I heard the sound of jingling bells coming closer to our gathering. A young woman with small brass bells on her costume and a pair of sparkly fairy wings jogged near us. She stopped when she saw us and stared. Then she took two steps forward and said, "Oooh, a baby!"

I held up Rhia and Rhia laughed.

The girl in the fairy wings bounced closer and said, "Hello, baby." Then she jogged past us, the sound of her bells jingling away into the darkness.

After a moment, Tama said, "Well, even the fairies welcome you."

Everyone laughed as Tama ended the ceremony with a cheerful, "Blessed be."

6

My brother's daughter Lindsay was born at the same hospital in San Francisco, five months after Rhia's birth. Lindsay's mom also had complications at the end of her pregnancy, but unlike Rhia, Lindsay was born strong and healthy. A plump, adorable baby with dark eyes and black hair, she was the complete opposite of thin, pale, and mostly bald Rhia. As they grew, the differences between Lindsay and Rhia became more obvious. Lindsay kicked and wiggled on strong, chubby legs. Rhia's legs stayed thin and didn't kick or wiggle as much. Rhia reached for a toy only when it was practically on top of her and then dropped it. She couldn't activate a switch on a talking toy or press a button on a BusyBox, all things Lindsay did successfully in the first six months of her life. A cold fear slowly grew in my core with every milestone Lindsay met and Rhia missed.

I learned to recognize the "she's a new mom" look on doctors' faces. A condescending smile, eyebrows drawn together as if seriously listening, a tilt of the head to relay compassion, and an almost indistinct tap of the foot or a pen. Then they would lean forward and say, "Babies grow differently. Give it time."

All their answers to try to calm my fear just made me doubt myself. They were doctors, the experts. I was a brand-new mom with zero experience. But despite my lack of experience with babies, I knew in my bones that something wasn't right about Rhia's development. I looked at Lindsay's strength and then felt the way Rhia's head flopped back when I picked her up, as if her head was too heavy to raise. Her grip on my finger when she nursed felt weak. When Rhia was seven months old she got a cloth baby book stuck on her head because she couldn't roll over to untangle herself. When she tried to crawl, she scooted on her belly with her butt in the air and inched forward, rubbing her face on the floor, never putting weight on her arms. And her blue eyes rhythmically twitched back and forth like the needle on a Geiger counter.

I felt that I was screaming and no one heard me: "Something is wrong with my baby."

"Everything is fine," the experts said.

"Something's wrong with my baby!"

"All babies are different."

"Something's wrong."

"Some babies reach milestones a little later than others."

"Something's wrong."

"You have a healthy baby."

"I know something is wrong."

"Give it time."

It was the wobbly eyes that finally convinced a doctor to send seven-month-old Rhia to a neurologist for a consultation. The elderly statesman-like expert walked into the room where Rhia and I waited, followed by a gaggle of white-coated student doctors. The statesman-neurologist examined Rhia as she lay on his white-paper-covered table, while he asked me questions. The students nodded and took furious notes. Then the statesman-doctor smiled with the same "there's nothing to worry about" expression as Rhia's pediatrician and announced that Rhia was perfectly fine.

"She's a little behind, but there's nothing to be alarmed by."

"Shouldn't she be able to roll over by now?" I asked, picking up Rhia before she started to cry.

"I checked her reflexes, her strength, and her coordination, and there is nothing I see that would impede her progress."

"Then why isn't she rolling over? Or pushing herself up? She should at least be able to push her own face off the floor."

"The only symptom of note is the nystagmus." He turned to his students. "The child's eyes still have a back and forth wobble, which should have resolved by three months of age."

The students scribbled more notes.

I asked, "Why hasn't it gone away?"

"That is usually caused by a problem with the eyes, not neurology. Vision problems can also cause physical delays like you see here." He pointed to Rhia and every student stared at her before scribbling more notes. The doctor said, "I will refer her to an ophthalmologist."

Her? He wasn't even talking to us anymore. Rhia was just an interesting case to teach his class.

The students smiled and nodded as they followed the statesman-doctor out the door, reminding me of a gaggle of white ducks.

The ophthalmologist declared that Rhia's vision was fine. Perhaps the nystagmus was caused by an inner ear problem, he suggested, referring her to an ear, nose, and throat specialist.

Laurent was worried, but I think he too wanted to alleviate my anxiety, so he tried to reassure me. His reassurances sounded too much like the doctors'. "They said there's nothing wrong. She's just developing slower."

"I know something is wrong!"

"But all the tests are normal."

"Then what's wrong?"

"Probably nothing. She's just weaker than other babies. But the doctors think she should catch up in time."

"You don't know that."

"I don't think we should worry yet."

Rhia was ten months old when she threw up while we were buying groceries at the supermarket. When the vomiting didn't stop after two hours, Laurent and I rushed her to the emergency room, where the doctor took one look at the nystagmus in her eyes and declared she probably had a brain tumor. Laurent and I both cried as we waited in the waiting room when the doctors took Rhia away for an emergency MRI, terrified that our worries had finally been acknowledged in the worst possible way. Two hours later I held Rhia tightly in my arms as the doctor gave us the results, no brain tumor.

He said, "She probably has an inner ear problem. Have you seen an ear, nose, and throat specialist?"

Rhia was sent home with anti-nausea medication and a referral to an ENT.

Laurent's parents hosted Rhia's first birthday at their house, and our whole family came, including cousin Lindsay. Seven-month-old Lindsay crawled on the carpet to play with Rhia's new toys, but Rhia still couldn't sit up without support from me to keep from falling backwards. Every person in that room tried unsuccessfully to hide their concern about Rhia. I looked at my mom, who quickly looked away. We all knew there was something wrong with Rhia, but no one wanted to admit the truth.

No one could now deny there was something wrong with my baby girl.

Fear

1

WHEN YOUR CHILD IS BORN WITH A DISABILITY, SOMEone will eventually quote the poem "Welcome to Holland," written by Emily Perl Kingsley in 1987. She wrote the poem to convey the confusion and loss that occurs when you become a special needs mom. She writes about planning a trip to beautiful Italy as a metaphor for preparing for the birth of a healthy baby. You learn the Italian language, study the maps, plan your route, and select the right hotels. You buy your ticket and then get on the plane heading for what you think is Italy. But when the plane lands, the captain says, "Welcome to Holland." Imagine the shock of landing in a country you hadn't planned for, and for some unknown reason, you can't get back on the plane and go to Italy like you wanted.

I hate that poem. I suppose it does a good job showing parents of "normal" kids the incredible stress that becoming a special needs parent causes, but it doesn't do much to help the parents sitting by an incubator praying their child learns to breathe on her own. Or the parents of kids who become violent when frustrated or have to wear socks on their hands so they can't scratch themselves until they bleed. "Welcome to Holland" encourages us to accept the change by enjoying the tulips and learning the language. I'm sure there are some special needs parents who can do that, but in my experience those families are few. I'm sure Ms. Kingsley meant the poem to be encouraging; unfortunately, too many family members and well-meaning friends have turned the sentiment into a Hallmark card by sending it to everyone with a disabled baby. I've received the poem five times.

Fuck you and your damn trip to Holland! I wanted to go to Italy!

My dreams of motherhood crashed to the ground, leaving shards of bitter glass all around that cut me deeply no matter how carefully I stepped. I kept waiting for happy milestones, like the first time Rhia would hold a spoon in one tiny hand or pull herself up in her crib. At that time, I was too frightened to see Rhia's own personal milestones, but when I look at her baby pictures today or read my journal, I see what I missed. For example, how she babbled nonstop in a language of her own while staring directly in my eyes as if expecting me to understand. I nodded and spoke back to her in English, and she watched my face as if absorbing every syllable. When she started talking in full sentences at eighteen months, I believed she actually had absorbed my words.

Rhia found her smile at three months old, filling the entire room with joy. She laughed in a high squeal of delight that fell into a chuckle lasting more than thirty seconds. She loved to be held and would cuddle against me with a happy sigh, sometimes looking up at me and smiling before snuggling even closer. Her favorite toy was a caterpillar stuffy with different textures and sounds on each segment of its plush body. She also loved picture books and begged to be read to by holding onto a baby book and pointing at the pictures. If you didn't sit beside her and explain what was on the page, she scowled at you with her eyebrows and lips scrunched tightly. When she was nine months old she learned to blow kisses by sucking in her cheeks while pursing her lips then smacking her mouth wide open. This was followed by her glorious smile.

I wish I could have focused more on those happy baby moments instead of drowning in the fear of knowing something was wrong with her. I missed the start of Rhia growing into her own, true, beautiful self.

2

My marriage to Rhia's dad collapsed at the same rate as my dreams of motherhood. It wasn't fair to him; he never claimed to be anything more than a Haight Street poet who loved me. When he became a dad, I expected him to change: stop smoking pot, get a "real job" with health insurance, and provide for his little family. He was happy smoking pot and playing video games with his buddies in between changing Rhia's diapers. He wanted to be her dad, while I wanted him to be her champion. I wanted a knight in shining armor who provided unlimited love and support, fought dragons, and kept us all safe. I could go along with our Renaissance Faire, Robin Hood fantasy for a while, but when Rhia's delays became apparent, I needed more. The fantasy was over, so I expected him to fight the medical system and demand real answers from the doctors. He didn't seem as afraid as I was, but of course that wasn't true; he was terrified. He just showed his fear differently than I wanted him to.

One night, after putting our sleepy daughter to bed, I found him at the top of the stairs leading to the basement. "Let's talk," I said.

He started walking down the stairs. "I'll be right back."

"No, really. I need to talk to you."

"Just a minute."

I knew he was going downstairs to smoke a bowl with our housemate and see the progress on the video game they'd been playing together. A minute would be a while. I walked into the living room, feeling the weight of loneliness and worry. Eventually I went to bed.

A few days later, I told him it was over.

He helped me pack. And then he drove Rhia and me three hours to my mom's house in Lake County.

After unloading the truck, he kissed his daughter goodbye.

"I hope this is what you want," he said without looking at me.

Living in a trailer park in Lake County with my mother was not something I wanted, but I didn't know what else to do. It was 1996 and San Francisco was too expensive for a single mom and her "failure to thrive" baby. What I wanted was my dream back, the one where my husband and I raise our daughter at the Renaissance Faire with the other faire brats.

I held back tears and said, "Thank you for your help."

He nodded once, then got back in the truck and drove away.

I know he cried all the way home.

3

WHAT DOES THE WORD "THRIVE" MEAN? WE USE THAT word to describe healthy houseplants and happy careers. The word is also used in advertising and is currently a logo for an insurance company. But what does it actually mean?

The word thrive is a verb, which means it requires action. We say "to thrive" and "thriving" because we only thrive when we are engaged in some kind of growth. The growth can be spiritual or physical, but thriving requires intent and energy. Thrive is not a noun; no one thrives by sitting still.

If "thrive" means to grow and learn, what does "failure to thrive" mean?

Lindsay could do all the things that a one-year-old was supposed to do. She could pull herself up to stand firmly on her strong legs, throw a ball at her older brother, and pull the clothes off her favorite doll. She could also climb out of her crib despite how much her mom told her to stay put. When Rhia and her cousin sat side by side on my mom's couch to look at books or watch a movie together, the difference between them was startling. I knew Rhia wasn't hitting eighteen-month-old milestones, but when I compared her wobbly eyes, low muscle tone, and poor coordination to the strong musculature of her younger cousin, I winced with dread.

My sister-in-law recommended I take Rhia to her own children's pediatrician for an evaluation. I wasn't sure what more he could offer compared to all the doctors at UCSF, but I was willing to try.

The small-town doctor took one look at Rhia and asked, "What kind of drugs were you taking while you were pregnant?"

I was so stunned it took several seconds to respond. "What? None! I never took drugs!"

I'm not sure he believed me. "Something is clearly wrong with your child." He pushed his glasses back up his nose and stared at Rhia thoughtfully. "Rhia was seen by a neurologist?"

"Yes. At UCSF."

"And they said there wasn't anything neurologically wrong?"

"Nothing. They thought it was her eyesight."

He just shook his head and mumbled, "Figures." While walking across the room to a display of paper pamphlets, he said, "I'm going to refer Rhia to Easterseals. They'll help her catch up developmentally." He handed me a bright yellow, tri-folded pamphlet with a picture on the front of a smiling child in a wheelchair and the words EASTER SEALS OF LAKE & MENDOCINO COUNTIES.

"What do I need to do?" I asked.

"Nothing. They'll call you to schedule an evaluation once I make the referral. It shouldn't be more than a couple of weeks before someone calls. If they don't call, let me know."

"Thank you," I said, feeling gratitude all the way to my core; maybe something could be done to help Rhia catch up to her cousin. I doubt he believed me about not doing drugs, but I didn't care. Let him think the worst! He was the first doctor who listened to me when I asked for help, and he was the first doctor who treated Rhia like a person rather than a specimen.

4

If enough therapy is thrown at a child early in life, then a disability can be overcome, and a lifetime of challenges can be avoided. That is the idea behind early intervention.

Once the doctor declared there was indeed something wrong with my baby, the agency onslaught began. Being unemployed became a good thing. It felt like everything went from 0 (nothing is wrong with Rhia) to 60 (everything is wrong with Rhia), making us both dizzy from the speed.

The pediatrician referred Rhia to Easter Seals, and they in turn referred her to the Regional Center, California Children's Services, and the Blind Babies Foundation. All four agencies worked together to provide "early intervention therapy." The theory is that if you give enough highly intensive occupational, physical, visual, speech, and behavioral therapy to a child before age three, then developmental delays can be overcome and the negative impacts of a possible disability lessened. This gave us a year and a half to fix Rhia's weak muscle tone, poor coordination, and sensory integration difficulties and also to resolve the hidden impact her impaired vision might have on her cognition.

Janet, the early intervention therapist, came to the house and played with Rhia twice a week. Of course, Rhia loved it. What toddler wouldn't love a one-on-one playmate who brought new toys and games every time? The two sat side by side on a soft blue blanket spread on my mother's living room floor, stacking colorful wooden blocks, singing silly songs, reading sturdy cardboard books, and coloring blank paper with fat crayons that were easy for a toddler to grip. I was expected to join in and learn how to play. I longed to tell Janet that I knew how to play and what I really needed was a nap, but I dutifully sat on the floor beside them and watched.

One day I asked, "Do you have to show a lot of parents how to play with their kids?"

"A lot of parents with drug-exposed babies don't know how to play with them," Janet said. Then her eyes opened wide as she quickly said, "Not that Rhia is drug-exposed! I didn't mean that. Not at all. I mean, a lot of kids I work with are drug-exposed—but not Rhia." She grabbed one of the board books and turned toward Rhia, saying, "Story time!"

Rhia threw a crayon at Janet.

The rumor that I was a drug addict had obviously spread. Was it written in Rhia's chart somewhere? Rhia rested against Janet while they read and occasionally she pointed at the pictures before smiling up at Janet. Rhia was happy, so I'd ignore how people assumed I was a drug addict simply because no one could explain the cause of Rhia's delays. Blaming the mom is always easiest.

Occupational therapy and physical therapy weren't as much fun as playing with Janet.

Occupational therapy (OT) focused on how Rhia used her hands and how her brain then processed sensory information. She was encouraged to press her hands into a large bin full of rice to find a favorite plastic toy buried in the grains (she refused to try). She was coaxed to play with Play-Doh, which she disliked, and shaving cream, which she absolutely hated. Rhia was labeled "tactilely defensive" because touching anything sticky, tacky, sandy, or prickly horrified her. She kept her hands in her lap as much as possible, and when she was eventually coaxed to hunt for a small, glittering pink ball buried inside a wad of gray Silly Putty, she jerked her hand away as if she'd been burned. Even touching chocolate pudding made her cry.

In speech therapy Rhia blew bubbles and used a straw to blow a cotton ball across a tray. Rhia could talk, but her weak mouth muscles made some of the sounds difficult, like S and L. This also made her at high risk of choking on food.

Physical therapy (PT) was more fun, but also challenging. At age two, Rhia still crawled everywhere and only stood while holding on to something, thus earning the new label "hypotonia," meaning her muscles were "floppy" and weak. Rhia folded herself into a pretzel while watching TV, legs bent backwards and her head poking through to see the screen, but she couldn't stand firmly on her own two feet without falling down. Rhia's favorite activity during physical therapy was bouncing on a large rubber ball, which increased her overall tone and trunk strength. First Rhia sat upright and bounced, giggling the entire time. Then she moved onto her belly, held up her head and arms, and then flew "like a fairy" while the PT rolled the ball side to side. The PT also showed me how to help Rhia push up from the floor by supporting Rhia's elbows close to her body and then encouraging her to look up at me.

The day Rhia pushed her chest up off the floor and looked up at me with her glorious smile felt better than any gift I could imagine!

The concern was real; if Rhia didn't increase her muscle tone, she'd never walk, feed herself safely, or speak clearly. So every therapist gave us homework:

- Play on the floor.
- Encourage Rhia to cross "midline" for brain development.
- Make her eat with her hands.
- Talk about the world using descriptive words and make sure she notices.
- Have cotton ball races by blowing through a straw.
- Bounce her on your lap.
- Lean side to side so she has to catch herself.
- Stack blocks to encourage coordination.
- Sing songs, the louder the better.
- Flop on a big bean bag.
- Have her push against you to increase her muscle tone.

I did everything they said. If my daughter could be helped, I would be the one to make it happen. We would do all the exercises and go to all the appointments and I would fill out all the forms and answer all the questions and it would be all done *now*. Her disabilities would be overcome! There was no time to play; everything was therapy.

5

The government has determined that a person is "legally blind," and therefore disabled, if their vision is worse than 20/200. Normal vision is 20/20. Rhia's vision was 20/1000, which meant that something twenty feet from Rhia would look like it's a thousand feet away. Details vanish, making Rhia's world one big, colorful blur of movement and noise. She was far more than legally blind; Rhia was considered functionally blind.

For some unknown reason, Rhia's optic nerves did not fully develop in utero, which is called optic nerve hypoplasia. The optic nerves sit directly behind the eyeballs and relay the visual information the eyes gather to the brain. If they are damaged or malformed, the optic nerves are unable to correctly relay visual information. There will be gaps in signals, creating a vision impairment. Rhia's optic nerves are small and pale, meaning they did not correctly form during gestation. Her optic nerves also show signs of damage, which indicate something happened after her birth to further the visual damage that had already occurred.

The Blind Babies Foundation sent a vision specialist named Claudia once a week. A beautiful woman in her mid-fifties, she instilled absolute confidence the moment I met her.

"Children gain most of their knowledge about the world visually through what we call incidental learning," she explained. "So if there's a vision loss, they miss out on important details about their world. Our job is to make up for that loss."

Claudia pointed to a vase of flowers sitting on my mom's kitchen table. "Rhia may see the yellow of those flowers, but she won't be able to tell what kind of flowers, how many, or even if they really are flowers or something else. We need to show her the flowers, let her touch the stem and count the petals. She needs to smell them and confirm they're real. We need to verbally explain everything about a flower so Rhia understands that a flower is more than a yellow blur on her grandmother's table."

This was an intervention Rhia and I both loved. I had instinctually been talking to Rhia about the sights and sounds around us, so I simply increased the detail. We looked at individual leaves on trees and shrubs, hunted for rocks in gravel beds, and picked off individual flower petals to compare the size and shape. Instead of just talking about birds, I described the "small brown bird" and how it was "scraping on the ground for worms." One day I showed her a worm, and, after a lot of encouragement, she held one in her tiny hand as if it were made of glass. Then she laughed and said, "It tickles." This was also the first time she'd allowed anyone to put anything slightly damp or sticky on her hand. Early intervention appeared to be working.

Not all agencies are helpful; I swear some try hard to keep us from getting any help at all. The biggest battles I have fought were with the Social Security Administration.

Welcome to the dark pit of paperwork.

When Rhia was officially labeled visually impaired at age two, I was handed the first stack of paperwork required for Social Security Disability Insurance. Rhia qualified for Medicare and for financial help, but to get it I had to fill out what felt like a thousand pages of documentation in triplicate. Then I had to drag her to medical evaluations from doctors who looked at the paperwork, glanced at her, then told us we could leave. Once the paperwork was filed and the evaluations finished, she and I sat through two separate interviews in hot beige cubicles where we were asked the same questions over and over by bored social workers.

They denied her, of course.

"How can they deny documented evidence of a vision impairment?" I furiously asked Janet one afternoon.

Janet handed Rhia another crayon, then looked at me and sighed. "Don't worry. They deny everyone the first time."

"That's ridiculous! Why do they do that?"

"I don't know. They just do. Every family I've ever worked with had to appeal."

"Are they trying to drive us crazy?"

Janet shrugged. "Probably."

I have learned that this is a typical tactic of most agencies; make the process impossible so the person will go away. The only way you'll get what you need is if you refuse to give up.

Refusing to give up, I filled out the thousand forms all over again to appeal, and nineteen months later, Rhia's disability payments and Medicare were approved.

By Rhia's second birthday she had been seen by a new pediatrician, an ophthalmologist, a new neurologist, an endocrinologist, a cardiologist, a pulmonologist, and an orthopedist. We drove all the way to Oakland, about three hours away, where she endured prodding, poking, and more blood work. There seemed to be a new theory every month about what caused Rhia's symptoms. The new neurologist ordered a new MRI and discovered Rhia's cerebellum was damaged, which caused her uncontrollable trembling, known as ataxia. But what had caused the damage to her cerebellum? Would she outgrow her ataxia? Was she also cognitively impaired? Could her low muscle tone be improved with enough physical therapy? Would her vision worsen? Was her condition degenerative, or was it caused by an event in utero? I finally had the official acknowledgement from doctors that something was indeed wrong with my baby, but there were still too many questions about Rhia's condition. Would she die? Is there a treatment?

Parents like answers. I hunted for those answers on the internet, a proven way to make yourself terrified. Rhia's doctors were good, but they didn't know everything, and they certainly didn't know my daughter like I did. If there was a way to save her, I would find it.

6

On a cold November day in 1997, the phone rang for the third time in a few hours. I groaned; I'd already spent that morning scheduling physical therapy and a follow-up appointment with Rhia's neurologist and had just sat on the couch with a cup of tea. I grabbed my daybook and pen before reluctantly answering. But it wasn't another doctor or therapist. The person calling was a woman named Diane from the Early Start Family Resource Center.

The Family Resource Center (FRC) works with families of children who need early intervention. Parents provide peer support, guidance about available resources, and help navigating the onslaught of therapy. Only another parent can truly understand the challenges families cope with while raising a child with disabilities. It sounded exactly like what I needed at that moment, and I was hungry to talk to another parent of a special needs toddler. I made an appointment for her to come to my house the next day

Diane was tall, soft spoken, and a few years older than me. Two of her three children had a type of disability, the youngest ten years older than Rhia.

I poured her a coffee and we sat at my yellow kitchen table while Rhia played with her dolls on the living room floor.

"How are you doing with all of this?" Diane asked, waving her hand at a stack of medical reports in the middle of the table.

"Completely overwhelmed," I said. Then it all came out in a rush. I told her about the long drives to Rhia's doctor appointments, juggling multiple therapy sessions and keeping up with the homework from each therapist, my long nights on the computer looking for answers, and the never-ending flow of paperwork.

"I appreciate it, I really do, but I feel overwhelmed by it all sometimes. Like every moment of Rhia's life is supposed to be some kind of therapy. And if I don't do it, she'll never walk or feed herself or be ready for school . . . or on and on, and I know they're right, but when do I get to just be her mom, you know?" I took a sip of my coffee to clear the tears in my throat, then continued. "I love that they're helping my daughter, but keeping track of it all and managing all that extra paperwork is too much sometimes. Instead of being Rhia's mom, I'm her caseworker!"

"I remember," Diane said. "I was completely overwhelmed too."

Because she too was a parent, she let me keep talking, pouring out every fear I felt in that hour we spent together. When I finally took a deep breath and we sat in silence for a moment, Diane quietly asked, "What do you want for Rhia?"

I stared at her. No one had ever asked me that before. "What do you mean?"

Diane leaned forward, resting her elbows on the table. "There are a lot of people telling you what they think your child needs, but what do you think she needs?"

I just shook my head. "I have no idea."

"It's okay. You don't have to know right now. Just think about it."

She told me about some of her own challenges with therapy and schedules, and by the end of her visit we were swapping recipes like old friends. But I kept thinking about her question: What do I want for Rhia?

That night, lying in my bed, I knew.

I want Rhia to be happy.

I want Rhia to go to school and learn and have friends.

I want Rhia to be able to eat safely.

I want Rhia to be healthy.

For six months, Rhia and I had done everything the therapists and doctors told us to do. That was fine because Rhia needed immediate intervention. But Diane reminded me it wouldn't be like that forever. Eventually, Rhia would go to school. There would be less urgency and more opportunity to include what I wanted for Rhia.

Eventually, Rhia could say what she wanted for herself.

7

I HAVE FRIENDS WITH CHILDREN CLOSE TO RHIA'S AGE, and I couldn't help but compare them. My friends took their children on trips, went camping, and watched their children perform in school plays.

My friends talked about how their children were in a dancing troupe or learning a musical instrument.

My daughter and I stayed home.

So what? Rhia and I were fine together and would create a new life, just the two of us. She loved to sing, so I taught her songs. She loved to dance, so I held her hands to help her stay balanced. She loved long walks in her stroller, so we went on adventures and looked for "signs of spring." She loved people, so we made new friends: the baker at the local cafe, the check-out clerk at the grocery store, the librarian. She loved books, so I made up stories. It wasn't a "normal" life, but it was still a good one. She was happy.

I was pretending to be.

Rhia and I went to a birthday party when a friend's daughter turned five. As the children played with the birthday girl's new toys, I stood near several mothers who were bragging about their toddlers.

"My son took three steps all on his own!"

"Well, Michael cruised all around the living room and even let go of the coffee table."

"My daughter climbed out of her crib all by herself! Can you believe it?"

The moms looked at me for a brief moment, waiting for my own story of Rhia's achievement, then quickly looked away and resumed bragging about their children.

What could I say? "My daughter is two and learned to sit up on her own after a year of physical therapy." It's just as much of an achievement as their children's. If they saw how much Rhia struggled to push herself up on her tiny arms and crawl to me, they would cheer just as loudly as they did when little Michael cruised the living room.

Parents mark off baby milestones like a developmental advent calendar, watching with glee how their children grow. I saw them as big red markers showing everything "wrong" with Rhia. She's two; why isn't she standing yet? Must be a problem with coordination/trunk strength/joint stability. She's three; why isn't she walking? Must be a continuing problem with coordination/trunk strength/joint stability. Or maybe tight hip flexors? She needs more therapy!

Rhia was advanced in one area: talking. It was as if she put all her energy into learning communication to make up for her struggling body. She talked in two-word sentences by age one, putting words together that made sense ("Go up."

"Want milk." "No sleep."). As soon as she learned a few words she talked to everyone about everything. It didn't matter if she knew a specific word or not; she had a way of making herself understood. I loved the sound of her baby voice as she talked, stringing words together like a Beat poet. Rhia used metaphors instead of simple sentences. "Up like a mountain" meant something was on a top shelf and out of reach. "Too under" meant the thing she wanted was below something and too hard for her to get without falling over. She said, "Don't work," when something was hard to do and, "It's impossible," when she was too tired to try. I didn't realize I used the word "actually" too much until she began using it in every sentence.

But one night when she was nineteen months old, the poetry suddenly made sense.

Rhia sat in her car seat in the back seat as I drove us home, chanting, "Mama. Mama. Mama . . ." Then I noticed she was talking about what was happening in the car.

"Mama is over there driving the car and I'm in back sitting. Mama is in front and I am in back. Front, back, front, back . . ."

Wait a minute . . . do toddlers know how to speak using correct grammar? I quickly looked over my shoulder at my tiny girl in her blue jumper, looking more like a baby than the toddler she was. She was talking to her hand like it was a puppet. "Mama and me. Mama drive us home. I am in the car. Mama and me. I am going home . . ."

I felt an immense sense of pride. Maybe Rhia couldn't stand up or cruise the furniture, but she could talk circles around other toddlers!

I am a huge bibliophile, so Rhia was one too. By age two she had more books in her bedroom than most adults have in their entire house. She memorized every word I read to her and recited the books to herself as she "read," using the pictures to remind her what the words on the page were. It was astonishing how accurate her memory was. If I missed a word or tried to summarize a long story, she protested immediately. "That's not what it says!" And she never forgot the words. Ten years later I have listened to her recite the written words of a favorite story and not miss a single one.

8

In many ways, Rhia was exactly like other toddlers. Rhia fought potty training, just like her cousin Lindsay did. My mom told me to put cotton panties on her so she would be uncomfortable when she wet herself. It didn't faze her. Rhia just stopped what she was doing, looked at me, and said, "You have to change me." Once she was clean she'd go right back to playing. The only person bothered by wet panties was me. I'd rinse them out, wipe up the pee that always got on the floor, and wonder what new bribe would lure her to the potty chair.

She also had tantrums like any typically developing toddler. I thought I was lucky when she breezed through the so-called terrible twos with hardly a whimper. But when she turned three it was like someone pushed the demon button on my sweet little girl. On the day before her birthday she happily raised her arms for me to place her in the high chair for dinner. On the day after her birthday she kicked and screamed and tried to bite me. Bath time became a battle of wills. She screamed while I undressed her and screamed louder when I put her in the tub. Once in the tub she played with her bath toys but wouldn't hold still for me to wash her hair. When bath time was over she screamed she didn't want to get out. She screamed as I pulled her slippery body out of the tub and screamed as I dried her off and got her dressed.

Every single day she fought me about something simple, like fastening the Velcro on her sandals. She wanted to do everything herself, which my mother said was what every three-year-old wanted. But unlike other three-year-olds, doing everything herself was harder for Rhia. So she screamed.

"Stop fighting with her so much," my mom said. "You can't win. She's three."

"She needs to listen to me," I said, folding my arms in exasperation.

"Why? Just do what you need to do and don't yell back. She's baiting you."

"Baiting me? How?"

My mom smiled like she knew a secret. "The next time she yells at you, don't react. Just watch."

After my mom left, I told Rhia it was time for dinner. She started kicking me the moment I picked her up. Instead of yelling at her to stop I just put her in her high chair and walked away. When I set her pink plastic bowl of cooked carrots and chicken in front of her, she yelled, "No!" and shoved the bowl off her tray. It landed on the ground with a loud clatter. Rhia looked at me with three-year-old triumph on her face. Remembering my mom's advice, I didn't yell. I walked away.

Rhia sat there with a wide open mouth, watching me go. Clearly, this wasn't what she expected. I was supposed to yell at her, not ignore her. I returned with a cloth to clean up the mess, then walked away again, leaving her in the high chair. After a few minutes Rhia said, "Mama."

"Yes, Rhia?"

"I'm hungry."

I brought her another bowl of cooked carrots and chicken. She happily ate every bite.

I had finally won a battle with my daughter.

A few days later Rhia almost knocked her bowl off her tray, this time accidentally.

I caught it and slid it back upright. "Ugh . . . be careful."

Rhia looked at me thoughtfully, then asked, "Why does 'ugh' mean be careful?"

I hadn't realized I'd said "ugh" until she mentioned it. "Hmmm. Well . . . 'ugh' is a surprise word. I thought your bowl was falling, so I said it. And then I said 'be careful' because I caught it."

She nodded and returned to eating her apple slices.

Seeing that my curious, intelligent child still lived inside the screaming toddler Rhia had become made me smile. Those moments between the battles were precious.

My mom had been right. Rhia not only threw tantrums because she was three but she also deliberately yelled at me because she seemed to enjoy making me mad. She wanted control, and making me mad was the ultimate control; she won every time she made me furious. When I stopped fighting back, she seemed disappointed and sometimes tried escalating the conflict by increasing the volume of her scream or breaking something. Occasionally she went too far and I would yell at her, but when I did I'd catch her looking at me with the tiniest gleam in her baby blue eyes.

Sometimes I was reminded how much information Rhia missed. One day when Rhia was almost three, she stared at her bowl of yogurt for a long time, then asked, "If yogurt is white, and ice cream is white, and mashed potatoes is white, how do you know which one it is?"

I laughed. I couldn't help it. It was such a surreal question, but she looked at me so studiously I realized it was an important question to her.

"Um . . . well . . . you can smell them," I said.

She sniffed her yogurt. "Smells like yogurt."

"Exactly. If we had any ice cream you could smell that and see how it's different."

Nodding, she kept looking at me, waiting for me to go on.

"And if we had any mashed potatoes, you could smell those and see how they're different from yogurt and ice cream."

"But what if you can't smell them?"

"Um . . . you can taste them. Also, mashed potatoes are usually hot and ice cream is usually cold. And yogurt is cold too, but not as cold as ice cream."

She took another bite of yogurt and then looked at me again, waiting.

"And you store them differently. Ice cream is in the freezer, yogurt is in the fridge, and mashed potatoes are cooked on the stove."

She nodded again, took another bite, then gazed off into the distance as if pondering my explanation.

How did she not know this? I mean, really . . . isn't the difference between ice cream, yogurt, and mashed potatoes obvious?

Not when you're visually impaired. Everything Rhia knows has been shown to her through explanation, direct contact, and hands-on experience. She couldn't sit in her chair and watch me cook dinner; she needed to be near me as I explained every step of a meal's preparation.

What is the difference between mashed potatoes, yogurt, and ice cream? Seems simple, right? We all automatically know, through experience. But if you can't see clearly, you have to trust that someone is offering you what you asked for because you really don't know until you take a bite.

9

RHIA HAS TWO DADS, THE ONE WHO HELPED CREATE HER and the one who helped raise her.

After I left Laurent I spent a year focusing solely on Rhia. I wasn't interested in dating or looking for another partner; I was too busy single-handedly battling my daughter's disability and possible death. But then I gave a lap dance to an old friend at a wake and everything changed.

It was 1997 when an acquaintance of mine died suddenly from a brain aneurism. My friends were devastated, so even though I wasn't close to the deceased, I went to the wake to support them. After leaving Rhia with Laurent in San Francisco, I caught the bus to the Tenderloin and then walked one block to Edinburgh Castle, a pub on Geary Street. I walked through the door into warm air smelling of tobacco, clove cigarettes, and marijuana. A song from the Pogues blasted from the speakers that were chained to the ceiling. The place was packed with people I knew from my life before I became Rhia's mom. In my battered Doc Martens and black leather jacket, I felt like myself again.

"Terena!" Teresa, a tall woman with long black dreads, hugged me, then led me to the bar. After downing a shot of Irish whiskey, I followed her outside, where we shared a cigarette.

Again, I heard someone yell my name. Looking up the street I saw three friends who I hadn't seen in years walking toward us. One of them was Rick.

After exchanging hugs, I said, "It's so good to see you all again, but I wish it wasn't for a wake."

We talked about our friend and the tragedy of his sudden death at age twenty-nine, then went inside to the bar together. While waiting for our drinks, Rick leaned closer to me and shouted, "I heard you moved back home."

"Yeah. Lakeport."

"How's it going?"

"Let's just say I'm happy to be here, even if it is for a wake."

Rick leaned toward the bar to grab the two pints of Guinness we'd ordered and handed me one. "Cheers," he said, clinking our glasses together.

Over the next couple of hours, I chatted with many old friends but kept circling back through the crowd to Rick. He bought me another Guinness and we talked about my divorce and his ex-girlfriend. When a chair near us opened, he offered it to me, but I preferred to stand. He sat down so I leaned closer to hear a story about his pet rat, when a very drunk Teresa suddenly picked me up and plopped me onto Rick's lap. She pressed up against us and shouted, "Give him a lap dance!"

Rick threw up his hands as she and I wiggled together to a Poxy Boggards song for about ten seconds before we collapsed into laughter. I pushed her off me, stood up, and hugged her tightly.

"God, I love her!" I said as I watched her skip into another group of friends.

"Me too." Rick said. Then he grinned. "After that, it would be rude if I didn't give you my number."

I had known Rick for five years and always thought he was sweet. A large, blond man with curly hair and a crooked smile, he was an acrobat in a small local circus. He also put on underground circus shows called Captain Rick's Toe Ring Circus. His signature act was to balance a running electric lawn mower on his chin while people threw heads of cabbage into the blades to make "coleslaw." His physical strength and sense of humor were sexy, but I hadn't let myself think about that when I was with Laurent. But now I was divorced, so I wrote down my number on a soggy bar napkin and told him not to lose it.

Our first date was awful; he spent most of the time talking about his ex-girlfriend and his bad luck with women.

When I dropped him off at his house, I held out my hand for him to shake and said, "Goodnight."

Taking my hand, he quietly said goodnight then left quickly. His shoulders slumped as he walked to his front door and he didn't look back as I drove away. But I decided to give him another chance because I'd known him to be intelligent and funny. The next time I brought Rhia to the city to visit her dad, I called Rick and asked if he wanted to go out. He managed to find two tickets to Cirque du Soleil the night

I would be in town, and this time he didn't talk about his ex-girlfriends. We hugged goodbye this time.

On our third date we went out for Thai food, but this time I was nervous. The third date is known as the "sex date," and I wasn't sure I wanted to sleep with him. He was kind, funny, and sexy in a Nordic Viking way, but we'd been friends for so long I wasn't feeling that spark. After dinner we walked to the house where I was staying. Was I supposed to invite him in? What if he wanted to stay? I turned to say goodnight when we reached the front door, and as I reached out to hug him, he suddenly wrapped his arms around me and kissed me. It was surprising, but lovely. I kissed him back, feeling every bone in my body tingle. That one kiss lit a spark, and he went from friend to potential lover in an instant.

He smiled, said goodnight, and walked away.

We talked on the phone several times over the next month, and when I was in San Francisco again, I stayed with him rather than at my friend's house. Sleeping in his arms felt good and safe, but I still didn't want a relationship. Sex, yes; but love . . . no. Love was complicated, and my life was complicated enough. Besides, I lived over two hours away from him. A long-distance relationship felt too hard.

We had dated for three months when he asked if he could meet Rhia.

When Rhia met Rick for the first time she stared at him from the safety of my arms.

"Hello," Rick said. "You must be Rhia."

In Rick's room, I sat on his bed with Rhia in my lap. "Rhia, this is my friend Rick."

Rick squatted down next to us and said, "It's nice to meet you, Rhia."

Rhia looked at him silently for a moment then leaned closer and put her tiny hands on his arm.

"Hi," Rick said.

Rhia grinned. She wiggled away from me, and Rick picked her up in his strong arms. She looked directly into his face and smiled again, then grabbed his goatee in one fist. It was clearly love at first sight.

Damn, I thought.

Rhia and I finally moved out of my mom's house and into our own place the summer Rhia turned two. Rick helped us move, and then he started driving up to Lake County almost every weekend. Rhia adored him; the moment she saw him walk through the front door she yelled, "Ricky!"

When my heart leapt at the sound of his car in my driveway on a Friday night, the feeling of happiness was quickly replaced by the fear of knowing I was in love with him. I wanted him, but I wondered if he truly grasped Rhia's disabilities and the incredible amount of focus and energy it took to care for her.

10

RHIA HAD BEEN IN THE EARLY INTERVENTION PROGRAM for a year and a half, and I finally felt comfortable managing the therapies and specialists. Then everything changed. At the stroke of midnight on Rhia's third birthday, she aged out of Early Intervention and moved into Early Start. Early Intervention was for babies and toddlers who needed therapy to catch up to their peers. Early Start was for children ages three to five who needed therapy to get ready for kindergarten.

But before she turned three, she had to be formally assessed by the Regional Center to determine if she qualified for more services or if the early intervention program had saved her from "mental retardation." That term was still in use in 1998, and many of Rhia's medical reports prior to 2005 have mental retardation as one of her labels. Today the label is developmentally delayed or developmental disability.

I debated the value of the cognitive assessment the Regional Center used: a problem-solving test with lots of pictures created for children with good eyesight. How accurate would the information be if Rhia struggled to see the images? I considered denying the assessment, but then Diane reminded me that the Regional Center paid for a lot of the therapy Rhia might need in the future, as well as vocational and recreational activities. If I refused the test, that money would disappear. So I signed the form allowing Rhia to take an IQ test she couldn't see given to her by an old man who'd never worked with a visually impaired child.

Mental retardation frightened me. I had learned to cope with Rhia's physical disabilities, but an intellectual disability was too terrifying to consider.

When I was a child in the 1970s, my father worked for the state hospital system, a program of hospitals and institutions for people who were unable to live on their own or take care of themselves. This included the mentally ill, severely disabled, and "mentally retarded." I remember visiting him at Sonoma State Hospital, a sprawling institution with beautiful, old buildings and immaculate green lawns where the "retarded" and "feeble minded" lived. Some of the people who lived there arrived as babies in the 1920s and fifty years later were still there, cut off from their families and the outside world.

It looked peaceful and beautiful, and I knew that some of the people lived in nice, apartment-style residences and had jobs within the institution, as well as a thriving social life. Many were happy. But the people my father worked with lived in the "gorilla ward." These were large, fully grown men with the intellectual abilities of a toddler, who were prone to outbursts and sudden violence. One day when we had lunch with Dad, a patient broke into the cafeteria and began throwing chairs and overturning tables. It took several of the workers, my father included, to restrain the man, inject him with a sedative, and carry him back to his room. My mom, brother, and I hid under a table, and after that event we never went inside the building for lunch again. I remember sitting in the car looking at the bars on the windows of the stone buildings and thinking of all the people inside who never left. I was nine years old, but I understood they were in a type of jail because they were disabled.

I remember that when I was growing up, children with disabilities went to school separate from us "normal" kids. There was no inclusion, no play buddies, and no lunch partners. We so-called normal students never interacted with a student with a disability. Occasionally we saw them on the far side of the sports field, or on the Special Bus traveling to their own, separate field trip. Kids with disabilities had to be protected from typically developing students, and young children had to be kept away from kids with disabilities so they wouldn't copy "abnormal" behavior.

I didn't want that life for Rhia.

Rhia was asked to point to the picture of a duck and then to point out the babies. She was asked to put a series of events in order using pictures. It was an absolutely ridiculous test for a blind child, so of course the IQ score came back "retarded." I didn't know if I should fight the score or let it stand.

I reluctantly accepted the "retarded" label so my child would get everything she needed. The Regional Center had a wealth of resources that could help her, especially as an adult, so why turn them down? But I sealed her actual IQ score in her records so no one, not a teacher, doctor, or therapist, would know it. I'd seen too many people give up on children when they thought the child couldn't learn. My daughter could learn; she was just slower.

I told this story to a colleague several years later, and she said, "Wow. You're a true optimist. I bet if someone dumped a huge pile of shit in your yard, you'd be happy for the compost."

"My daughter taught me to be flexible," I replied.

After the Regional Center assessment, Rhia needed more assessments for her physical, behavioral, and educational abilities. Just like at the beginning of the early intervention process, the phone rang every day with another specialist wanting to observe and/or assess Rhia's needs. She also needed health and vision tests. Her vision impairment meant she qualified for instruction by a teacher of the visually impaired. Rhia also qualified for school-based physical therapy and occupational therapy. When all of the assessments were finished and reports with recommendations had been completed, a social worker from the school district called to schedule the IEP. As soon as I hung up the phone I went online to figure out what the letters "IEP" stood for.

An IEP is an individualized education plan, which lays out all of the services and supports a child with a disability needs to succeed in school. That's why there were so many assessments before preschool. Goals were written by all of those specialists and educators based on certain deficits their assessments found. For example, Rhia would need assistance finding all the various locations in her new classroom because her vision impairment meant she couldn't just look around and find the books. Someone would need to show her where the books were and how to safely get there. That person would be her orientation and mobility teacher. Rhia had trouble walking up and down steps, so someone needed to walk with her for safety. The physical therapist would work on that skill so that eventually Rhia could walk up two steps on her own. Not only were specific goals written, but the amount of time she would have with each specialist had to be figured out. Would Rhia need two hours of PT each week to meet her goal, or could she do it with one hour of therapy? Whatever was written in the IEP documents became the contract, and the school district was legally required to provide those supports.

Diane from the Family Resource Center offered to come with me to the first IEP meeting. "No one should go to these meetings alone. They can be overwhelming." Gratefully I accepted her help.

The IEP meeting was held in a beige conference room with no windows and in the center a large, round table with comfortable black chairs. Ten people sat at the table, most of them specialists, plus one administrator from the district. The administrator, a large man with gray hair, stood and shook my hand to welcome me to the circle. I was handed a large stack of documents, the IEP itself.

Without Diane taking notes and asking questions, I would have been lost. I tried keeping up as the "IEP team" threw jargon around and discussed terms like "benchmarks," "frequency," and "outcomes." The school district in the next town had a special needs preschool that sounded perfect for

Rhia's needs, so I agreed to send Rhia there. She would get the one-to-one attention and therapy she needed to prepare her for kindergarten, and she'd get to spend the day with other children, something she hadn't experienced in Early Intervention.

The meeting ended, and even though Diane had told me I didn't have to sign the forms right away, I signed them anyway. With my signature I was agreeing to the proposed goals, therapies, and school site written in the document.

Rhia was ready for preschool.

Rhia bounced and sang in her car seat as I drove her to school on her first day. She had never spent more than an hour or two away from me.

"Do I get to eat lunch at school, Mama?" she asked.

"Yes. You'll have lunch with your new friends."

"But I don't got lunch."

"Your school has lunch for you."

"Will I like it?"

"I'm sure you will."

"What if I don't like it?"

"You can have more lunch at home."

After parking the car, I opened Rhia's door and helped her out. She gripped my hand tightly as we walked to the front of her school where her new teacher, Mrs. Grant, waited with several other small, squirrely preschool students. Rhia and I had met her several weeks earlier when we toured the school.

"Hi, Rhia. Are you ready to go to class?" Mrs. Grant held out her hand.

Rhia let go of my hand, took her teacher's hand, then she looked at me and waved as she walked away with her teacher. "Bye, Mama," she said.

Tears ran down my face as I watched my little girl start her first day of school with absolute confidence. She didn't cry or whine or beg me to come with her. She just took her teacher's hand and walked away.

I sat in my car and cried for an hour before I could leave.

Hope

"It would be funny if dogs could talk, because then they could tell me where they wanted to walk.

It would be funny if dogs had hands, they could draw a picture, but they might eat the crayons."

—Poem by Rhia, age 6, with help from her mom.

1

Some people believe that a blind person with multiple disabilities doesn't need orientation and mobility lessons. After all, if they are developmentally delayed they'll need an aid traveling with them to keep them safe. The aid will intervene if there are obstacles, so spending time practicing orientation and mobility is a waste of resources.

But Laura, Rhia's orientation and mobility teacher, didn't think that way, and I am eternally grateful to her.

If you cannot see the environment you're walking in, how do you know where you are? How do you cross a street safely if you can't see the cars? Orientation and mobility, also called O&M, teaches people with vision impairments skills to travel safely by using landmarks and environmental clues. You may have seen the person walking along the sidewalk swinging a white cane with a red stripe back and forth in front of them. That person took orientation and mobility classes to learn how to use that cane properly. But there is more to O&M than just using a white cane to travel.

Rhia often used a stroller to travel from place to place simply because she lacked the stamina to walk more than a block or two. She would climb in with assistance, be buckled in, and then the stroller would be pushed to her destination. Once there, she'd hop out and hold a grownup's hand while they walked around the location together. When it was time to go, Rhia would return to the stroller and be pushed to the next place or back to where the journey began. Rhia's world was reduced to the confines of her red fabric stroller with the black buckle; how she got from point A to point B was a mystery.

It was Laura's job to end that mystery.

Rhia met Laura in the sandbox, her favorite place on the preschool playground. Thanks to early intervention therapy, Rhia tolerated the feel of sand and dirt. She played happily on her own within the confines of the sandbox, cheerfully digging holes with her fingers or pouring sand into a bucket and then tipping it over. The sandbox was safer than the open playground where the children raced each other on loud plastic tricycles or threw bouncy balls as hard as they could. Whenever she was asked what she wanted to do at recess, Rhia chose the sandbox with its square box shape and quiet toys and teachers who stopped the other students from throwing sand.

Laura wanted to show Rhia there were other activities on the playground that were fun, like the swings. But first Laura had to earn Rhia's trust and encourage her to try something out of her comfort zone. Every week Laura met Rhia in the sandbox during recess, at first building camaraderie and trust through play. After a month, Rhia allowed Laura to pick her up and carry her across the playground to see the swings. Laura brought Rhia back to the sandbox as soon as Rhia said she wanted to. The following month Laura sat on the swing with Rhia in her lap, not moving, but just showing Rhia how the swings worked. They explored the chains together with their hands and felt the hard plastic seat shaped like a car seat. Eventually, Rhia allowed Laura to help her sit on the swing on her own and be buckled in, but it took two months more before Rhia was okay with the swing moving. In the spring of Rhia's first year in preschool, she let Laura swing her gently five times. As soon as they counted five, Rhia declared she was done and wanted to return to the sandbox. To keep building trust, Laura did as Rhia asked.

During Rhia's second year of preschool, after the summer break, Laura found Rhia in the sandbox again. This time, Laura decided to introduce Rhia to the wagon. Because Rhia trusted Laura, she allowed Laura to put her in the wagon with the high back and pull her slowly around the playground. Eventually, the other children wanted to be pulled in the wagon, too, or to pull it with Rhia inside. Rhia gripped the plastic sides of the wagon and smiled while two children pulled her around the playground. It had taken a year and a half for Rhia, but she was finally included in a game with her classmates.

At the end of her second year in preschool, there was a party on the playground to celebrate the students who were graduating and going to kindergarten in the fall, Rhia included. It was a stifling hot day in June, which happens in Lake County.

The hills turn from green to gold as the grass dries up and the temperature climbs into the nineties Fahrenheit. One of the teachers brought a kiddie pool about the same size as the sandbox, and Rhia joined her classmates to splash in the water. Rhia sat and poured water in and out of a bucket, just as she had with sand.

One little boy kept taking off his swim trunks and jumping into the pool naked. A teacher grabbed him and put his trunks back on, but in five minutes he'd strip them off again. He jumped in the pool and stood next to Rhia, his tiny penis next to her head. As the teacher rushed to reprimand him, Rhia reached out and grabbed his penis in her fist and stood up, yanking him down hard until he sat in the water. The little boy yelled and started to cry. Rhia looked at him wondering what had happened. We adults couldn't stop laughing. Rhia needed to stand, so she grabbed the handle that was in her face, not realizing that "handle" was attached to a small, naked boy.

"Well," said one of the teachers. "I bet he keeps his shorts on now."

2

On a warm autumn day in 1998, Rick and I sat on my front steps and talked about the future while Rhia napped. The conversation started casually; Rick dreamed of owning his own property and wondered if Lake County would be a good place to buy land. We debated the pros and cons of various towns in the county and what kind of house he wanted. Then we started talking about how many bedrooms and which school district would be best for Rhia.

After a long pause in the conversation, Rick asked, "Are we talking about what I think we're talking about?"

"I think so," I murmured.

"Is that okay with you?"

I nodded. "Yes."

He took my hand and we sat together quietly for a while longer, lost in our own thoughts.

"I love you," he said.

"I love you too."

Rick and I couldn't become legally married because our combined income would have caused Rhia to lose her medical benefits. This is a problem for many people with disabilities and their families. Thousands of adults with disabilities are unable to marry, so they live together as spouses without the legal and financial privileges of marriage. If the choice is keeping or losing health insurance, most people choose to stay unwed.

That didn't stop Rick and me from having a ceremony in 1999 in Golden Gate Park; we just didn't file the paperwork. We were broke because Rick had just bought a small house in Lakeport, and every dollar we had went into the purchase and renovation. Again, that didn't stop the party. We invited our friends to join us for a communal picnic. Two friends donated a wedding cake and another brought a keg of beer. Several friends brought champagne to share. My good friend Ilona took the wedding pictures. My wedding gown was a pink satin, two-piece, vintage Chanel ensemble that reminded me of something Audrey Hepburn would wear. I paid fifty dollars for it, and another twenty dollars for a vintage straw hat decorated with black tulle. My bouquet was created from bouquets given to me by friends. Rick and I were married by my friend Rose, and Tama, my Renaissance Faire sister, was my bridesmaid. Four-year-old Rhia was the flower girl.

As Rose wove a red ribbon around Rick's and my intertwined hands during the ceremony, I heard several guests giggle. Then I heard whispers and more laughter. Tama nudged my arm and then pointed down to Rhia, who stood between us.

Rhia was bent over with her bouquet pulled apart, trying to stick the flowers into the ground.

"What are you doing?" I asked her.

"I'm putting the flowers back in the ground because that's where they go," she said while concentrating on shoving fragile stems into the hard, grassy ground.

After the ceremony, several of Rick's circus friends put on a circus show in our honor. My father even performed a magic act, and my friend Brigitte belly-danced with her troupe. The finale was when Rick and I walked through flaming batons thrown by two expert jugglers.

Before we entered the circle of flames, Rick took my hand and said, "Just follow my lead. When I say go, we go."

"Okay." I gripped his hand tightly and watched the flaming torches pass inches from our faces. I had decided to trust him with my heart and my daughter, so I would trust him to keep us from getting burned.

One of the jugglers gave a signal I didn't see and Rick said, "Go." We stepped forward together and stood inside the movement of the torches. Everyone cheered. The mysterious signal came again and Rick said, "Go." When we reached the other side of the flames, we kissed and laughed.

Rhia, Rick, and I were now one family, and we had walked through fire to prove it.

3

Laura wasn't the only one pushing Rhia to try new things; Rick was determined that Rhia escape her comfort zone. When we first started dating and he came up to Lakeport for visits, Rick brought her an oversized floor pillow stuffed with enough foam to keep a hundred-pound vase from shattering, let alone a twenty-pound child. He dropped it on the middle of my living room floor and then plopped himself on top of it. Rhia laughed, then wobbled over to him and plopped onto his stomach. He picked her up, rolled off the pillow, and plopped her onto it face first.

"Plop!" he said.

Rhia giggled, scooted off, stood up, and let herself drop back onto the pillow face first. "Plop!" she said, laughing so hard she rolled off the pillow onto the linoleum floor.

I fought the urge to run to her as Rick helped her sit up, rubbed the top of her head, and grinned. "You're okay. Try again." He fell back onto the pillow and said, "Plop!"

The "plop" game quickly became Rhia's favorite. When Rick left, she showed me how to play the game, and when I rolled off the pillow one time, she said, "You gotta stay on the pillow, Mama."

I had assumed that Rhia would be too frightened to play a rough and tumble game, but Rick showed me that Rhia was just like other kids. All kids love to climb and jump and test their limits. Rhia just needed a big pillow to land on.

Rhia loved running errands with Rick. He drove a 1981 Toyota truck with a stick shift and a camper shell on the back. Her car seat was secured in the center of the passenger seat, and she remembered not to kick the stick shift when she sat there. The two of them would go to the grocery store or Home Depot, Rhia waving and yelling, "Bye, Mama!" as they drove away.

One day all three of us prepared to run an errand together. I opened the passenger door and reached down to pick up Rhia, but Rick said, "She can do it."

I was confused. Do what? Open the door?

Rick said, "Rhia, climb in. Show your mom."

Rhia let go of my hand and reached up to grip the passenger seat with both hands. Then she put her knee on the floor of the cab and heaved herself up. I watched in amazement as she scrambled up onto the seat and then climbed into her car seat. She put her arms through the shoulder straps and grinned, obviously pleased with herself.

"I didn't know you could do that," I told her.

I sat beside her and buckled her in. Rick started the engine.

"When did she learn that?" I asked Rick.

"A few weeks ago. She figured it out herself. At first I told her to climb in and she stood there waiting for me to pick her up. When I didn't, she climbed in on her own. It took a couple of tries, but she did it."

"All alone?" My voice must have shown the images I had in my mind of Rhia falling out of the truck.

"I stood behind her at first and made a couple of suggestions, like what to try holding on to. But once she did it on her own I just tell her to climb in and then walk away."

I glanced at Rhia and then Rick. What other surprises did they have for me? I was so used to keeping Rhia safe, as most mothers do, that I forgot to let her explore. To just be a kid. Let her fall down and get bruises and bumps, just like other kids.

Rick also taught her how to tell a joke.

It was July in 1999. The three of us were cooling off inside the house, the swamp cooler doing its best to keep the room twenty degrees cooler than the hundred degrees outside.

Rhia sat beside Rick on the couch. He turned to her and said, "What's funnier, hot weather or cold weather?"

Rhia thought for a minute and then said, "Hot. Because it makes you sweaty."

"Good one!" Rick said, and they both laughed.

Then Rick pointed at our cat, Dharma, and asked, "What's funnier, dogs or cats?"

Rhia again thought for a moment, then she said, "Cats. They poop in a box."

They both laughed together loudly.

Rick asked two more "What's funnier" questions, then he said, "Your turn."

Rhia looked around the room and said, "What's funnier, my cup or your cup?" She pointed at his glass of Diet Coke.

Rick said, "My cup, because it makes me burp."

Rhia giggled. "Good one!" She pointed at me. "Your turn."

"Hmmm . . ." I said, looking around the room. "What's funnier, a cookie or a cracker?"

Rhia frowned. "They're the same thing."

I looked at Rick and said, "Clearly I don't understand the rules of this game."

He laughed and asked me, "What's funnier, a banana or an apple?"

"A banana."

"Right! Why?"

"Because they're slippery."

"Exactly. Now you get it." He said to Rhia, "Ask her another one."

Rhia thought for a few seconds, then asked me, "What's funnier, a pillow or a chair?"

"Ummm . . . a chair?"

Rhia sighed. "No, a pillow, because you can have a pillow fight." She looked at Rick and said, "Mama don't get it."

He laughed. "She just needs more practice."

We played the game often over the years, which helped Rhia's surreal sense of humor grow.

4

Inclusion (noun)

: the action or state of including or of being included within a group or structure.

: the practice or policy of providing equal access to opportunities and resources for people who might otherwise be excluded or marginalized, such as those who have physical or mental disabilities and members of other minority groups.

THE NEXT TIME YOU GO TO AN ELEMENTARY SCHOOL, look for the special education classroom. You'll usually find it in the back of the school grounds, far away from the main school building. It will probably be in a temporary classroom, as if the architects of the school forgot to include a special education classroom when the building was constructed. Even if there are other portable classrooms at the school, the special education classroom will be the one on the far end of a row or set completely separate from any other classroom.

Today, the classrooms are still separated, but there is more contact between typically developing children and special education children. When Rhia began kindergarten in 2001, special education students were completely isolated; they didn't even eat lunch at the same time as other students. It reminded me of the institution where my father worked.

I decided I wanted something different for Rhia.

Diane asked me to dream again, just as she had when I was overwhelmed by Rhia's Early Start program. She reminded me that rather than go along with whatever the school experts and teachers told me Rhia needed, I could have a say in how Rhia would be educated. I dreamed of a sunny kindergarten class with a kind teacher and a bunch of wiggly five-year-olds sharing their crayons with Rhia, just as her cousin Lindsay would have. I saw Rhia surrounded by friends who showed her how to be a regular kid, something that a child with a vision impairment desperately needed. Visually impaired children need to be taught how to interact with people and make friends; they can't just observe social norms. A dark special education classroom at the back of the playground wasn't part of my dream.

Deciding to fight for the dream, I asked Diane for help. She warned me it would be a battle. I looked up my rights as a special needs parent and studied special education laws. I learned that a special education classroom was not the automatic choice; the child's needs and educational requirements must be taken into account and a student's placement individualized based on those needs. After doing my homework, I thought I was ready for the fight with the school district.

I was wrong.

At the beginning of Rhia's IEP meeting to plan her first year of kindergarten, I said, "Rhia should be in kindergarten with typical five-year-olds, not stuck in a special education classroom."

"But she needs special education," said the elementary school principal, a white man in his mid-fifties wearing a suit and tie.

"Yes, she does, but why can't she have special education in kindergarten?"

"It is kindergarten. But in a separate room where she can have the one-to-one support she needs."

"I want her in a regular kindergarten class with the one-to-one support she needs."

"We only provide one-to-one aids in the special education program."

"Rhia is in the special education program, just in a different room. Why can't she have an aid?"

"Providing separate instruction with an aid for Rhia will be disruptive to the other students. We have to consider their needs as well." He leaned forward across the table and smiled kindly. "Go see the classroom. Meet the teacher. I think you'll be pleasantly surprised."

I looked at the other people from the district who were seated at the table. There was a regular education teacher, a speech pathologist, a physical therapist, and a school psychologist. Everyone nodded, except the PT, who looked down at the table.

Diane had advised me to be firm but cooperative, so I agreed to talk to the special education teacher. The IEP meeting was rescheduled for the following week, and then I walked across the playground to meet Vickie, the elementary school special education instructor who was teaching summer session.

She was a kind-hearted, large, grandmotherly type, obviously devoted to her students. I watched her read a book to five boys sitting on a bright red carpet with three aids nearby reminding them to be quiet and listen. There were no girls in the room. When the story was finished they went to the tables to work on an art project related to the book, again with assistance from the aids. Vickie (she preferred to be called Vickie rather than Mrs. Lopez) and I stepped outside to chat about Rhia.

As I talked to her about my dream for Rhia to have a typical kindergarten experience, I saw in Vickie's wide eyes and crossed arms that she didn't understand. She shook her head slowly and I sensed her thoughts: *How can Rhia learn in a regular education classroom? The poor dear will be lost.*

"It's so much better for my students if they are here in the classroom with me teaching them directly. My students have specific needs, just like your daughter, and that requires my supervision and support." Those were her spoken words, but what I felt she was saying was, *My students can't cope with any type of stress; they need protection, not inclusion.*

Vickie explained that the regular education teachers were hesitant to have children with disabilities in their classrooms because special education students often have outbursts that are disruptive to the other students. It was better for everyone if special needs kids were taught in special needs classrooms.

There was that word again: disruptive. Rhia was kind, quiet, loved learning, and had zero behavior problems. She would not be disruptive to anyone. And how much more disruptive was a kid with disabilities compared to any ordinary five- or six-year-old?

I returned to the district office for the second meeting and this time brought up the law regarding "least restrictive environment," a requirement under the federal Individuals with Disabilities Education Act that states children must be educated with their peers as much as possible. The principal discussed the need to keep Rhia safe and how that required extra staffing. I again mentioned least restrictive environment and requested a one-to-one aid. Then the school psychologist brought up the costs associated with hiring an extra aid, and that's when I had them; it is illegal to make special education decisions based on cost. When the district realized I knew the law and had done my homework, they reluctantly agreed to "give it a try."

I joyfully went school clothes shopping with my sister-in-law and niece. We bought Rhia and Lindsay matching blue shirts with little pink hearts on the sleeves. They were going to different schools in different towns, but would both be in the kindergarten class I dreamed of, and they were both completely adorable.

The idea of inclusion was a brand-new concept in education and completely unheard of in this elementary school. Rhia would be their test case. A one-to-one aid was hired, and Rhia started kindergarten in Room One with the regular education kindergarten class. Her teacher was kind and creative and worked hard to include Rhia in everything. The only drawback was the aid tended to do too much for Rhia. I got a lot of perfectly drawn, organized art projects that had obviously been done by the aid with Rhia "supervising." She didn't understand that Rhia's chaotic crayon strokes and unreadable letters were beautiful to me.

Rhia's orientation and mobility teacher, Laura, helped Rhia orient to her new school. She also brought Rhia a white cane to help her travel around safely. Rhia proudly held her white cane in one hand and Laura's hand in the other, keeping the cane tip down and showing off how quickly she learned to avoid curbs, dips, cracks, and anything else that could trip her. She also demonstrated how resilient she was when she discovered she could use her white cane to slow down other kids. Every recess, Rhia tried to keep up with her classmates on the playground, but since it took her so long to get anywhere, recess was almost over before she could join a game. One day during recess she stuck out her cane in front of a kid who was racing to the swings. When the kid fell, Rhia loudly said, "Gravity check!"

When the teacher told me I tried hard not to laugh. "Gravity check" was a personal joke between Rhia and me. Rhia fell often, so I began calling those incidents gravity checks. Whenever either of us tripped or fell, we'd yell, "Gravity check! Still working!" Rhia had decided it was funny to conduct her own gravity checks at school. She was reprimanded by her teacher and by me, but when she tripped a student again and quietly said, "Gravity check," to the child who was crying on the ground, Rhia's cane was taken away. Rhia would use the cane at home, during lessons with Teacher Laura, and while walking with an adult, but not on the playground.

I guess Rhia wasn't ready for a two-foot-long gravity check stick.

Kindergarten flew by, filled with learning and exploring. After Rhia accepted her certificate at kindergarten graduation, her teacher declared the full inclusion experiment a success. But at the start of Rhia's first grade school year, inclusion fell apart. Rhia was six years old and couldn't read her own name. Her educators and therapists worried that without separate instruction, Rhia would never learn to read. When I requested a one-to-one aid again, the district said the classroom teacher didn't want an aid working with Rhia at her desk because it would be disruptive to the other students.

Disruptive. I hate that word almost as much as "special."

The district and I compromised; Rhia would spend half of the day in the special education classroom doing academics and the other half in the regular education classroom for socialization and extracurricular activities. She would also begin braille instruction, because it had become clear that Rhia's vision impairment made even large print letters impossible for her to read. It was the best the school would offer without a lawsuit, and with Rhia so far behind academically, it made logical sense. With a deep sigh, I signed the IEP.

For a few months, the education plan appeared to work. Rhia began her school day in the special education classroom, where she finally learned to spell her name and count to one hundred. She liked Vickie, probably because Vickie coddled her. Rhia was a master at pouting when something felt too hard; she knew exactly how much to look tearful to get out of work. In the afternoon, Rhia went to her first grade class with her aid. The first graders thought she was adorable and sweet, and everyone wanted to be Rhia's helper.

Rhia received braille lessons with a teacher of the visually impaired twice a week. Lessons focused on increasing the sensitivity of Rhia's fingertips. Braille letters are created using two rows of three tiny dots in various patterns. A single raised dot in one row is an A, two raised dots in one row is a B, one raised dot at the top of each of two rows is a C, and so on. A braille reader needs very sensitive fingertips to understand what those tiny dots mean as they move their fingertips across a page that may have hundreds of dots. It takes years of practice, but it begins with learning to feel tiny details of small objects using only your fingertips. Rhia started by feeling plastic barnyard animals hidden inside a box and then tried to guess what they were. She thought the game was funny.

After two years of struggle, it became apparent that Rhia's hand tremors made reading braille impossible; she simply couldn't move her fingers across the braille bumps smoothly enough to feel the formed letters. Therefore, her education focused on increasing Rhia's auditory skills. A CCTV (close circuit television) was purchased by the district so that Rhia could enlarge the images and letters of her lessons during class.

Three months into the school year, I got a call from the principal. Rhia had thrown things in class and spat at Vickie. I needed to come to school immediately.

I was shocked. Rhia hadn't thrown anything since she was three years old. What happened?

Rhia was sitting in the office with an aid I didn't recognize. Vickie was waiting for me with the principal in his office. She said that Rhia had become angry when she wasn't allowed to go to the regular education classroom.

"Why couldn't she go?" I asked.

"Her aid is sick and I didn't have anyone to go with her," Vickie replied.

Rhia had tried to go out the door on her own but Vickie told her no. Rhia sat in her chair and when Vickie brought her coloring crayons and paper, Rhia responded by spitting on Vickie and throwing the crayons.

Vickie was furious. This was a woman who was always smiling and kind, like an aging *Romper Room* teacher. But now she glared at my daughter as if she'd like to spit back at her.

The principal said there would be a report written about the incident and placed in Rhia's permanent school record. She had earned the "behavior problem" label.

I took Rhia home and tried to figure out what had happened. Between sobs, Rhia explained that she was the "Shining Star" that week in her first grade class and they were doing a special activity that day to celebrate her. Kids had drawn pictures of Rhia, and her teacher had talked about how special Rhia was. On that day, they were giving her an award for being the "Kindest Kid."

Now I wanted to spit. How dare they punish a six-year-old by depriving her of being the Shining Star! No one had bothered to figure out why she was angry; they had just punished her for acting out.

The next day I met with the principal again and explained about the classroom and the Special Star. He sympathized but refused to retract the report. I insisted my objection be added to her file and then I went to see Vickie.

She was sitting at a table with two other students when I entered. "Did you know Rhia was the Shining Star?"

Vickie stood up slowly. "No. I didn't. But that doesn't excuse Rhia's behavior."

"You're right. Spitting isn't okay. But maybe you could try talking to her next time rather than making the situation worse."

"Are you blaming me?" She sounded incredulous.

"Yes. Rhia doesn't have behavior problems. She's never had an outburst like this in her entire life! I can't believe you didn't consider what might have set her off."

Vickie turned her back and walked away.

I stared at her as my anger turned into resignation. Vickie was in her late fifties and had probably been teaching for more than thirty years. She had her way of doing things, and the concept of inclusion was too far outside her paradigm to imagine. The only thing I felt I could do was get Rhia out of that classroom. But how?

Rick had the solution. He was working in Mendocino County, the county one hour away that had better schools and more resources.

"Let's move," he said. "Lake County has nothing for Rhia."

5

In 2002, we moved out of Lake County and into a three-bedroom house on Mill Street in Ukiah, just down the road from the movie theater. The neighborhood was known as the West Side, a highly desirable neighborhood with lots of trees and charming older houses. From our front door we could walk less than half a mile to the grocery store or to downtown shops. Rhia loved going for daily walks on the well-maintained sidewalks of Ukiah.

Laura lived a mile from our house and was thrilled Rhia was in the Ukiah school system. Ukiah was ahead of its time in terms of special education inclusion; the district believed that all students should be fully included in regular education classes and had hired an inclusion specialist to support the classroom teachers for greater success.

On the first day, Laura came to Rhia's new school to help Rhia orient to a whole new environment. She also gave a talk to the kids in Rhia's class so they would know how to be Rhia's friend.

"Rhia can see some," Laura said. "But you need to be close to her and go slow or you'll be a big blur."

A child raised her hand. "Why is it blurry?"

"Rhia's eyes don't get all the information they need because a part of her eyes isn't working right. So things look blurry to her. But she isn't totally blind, and she can see a lot if you help her."

All the children quietly nodded and glanced at Rhia, who was sitting at her desk pretending Laura wasn't talking about her. I stood at the back of the room, filled with hope that this sunny classroom with friendly children would help Rhia bloom.

During the second week of school, Laura and I observed Rhia again. Rhia sat quietly at a table waiting to go outside to play while her aid went to fetch Rhia's jacket.

"What are you doing?" Laura asked the aid.

"Getting Rhia's coat."

"Why are you getting it?" Laura asked.

"Ummmm . . ." The aid looked like she thought it was a trick question.

Laura said, "Rhia can get her own coat."

"It's okay. I don't mind getting it for her," the aid said with a smile.

"I know, but wouldn't it be great if Rhia could get her own coat?"

Laura went to the table and held out her hand for Rhia. "Hi, Rhia. It's Laura. Let's go get your coat."

Rhia looked at her for a moment, then got up and took Laura's hand. The two went to the coat rack together where Rhia's bright red coat hung.

"Which coat is yours?" Laura asked Rhia.

Rhia shrugged. "I don't know."

Her aid said, "It's the red one with the hood."

Laura smiled. "I see it. Let's figure out how Rhia can find it too." Laura and the aid chatted for a moment about moving Rhia's hook closer to the door and adding sparkle to her name tag so she could easily find it herself. Rhia hummed to herself while she waited.

Then Laura took Rhia's coat and said, "Here's your coat, Rhia."

Rhia held out her arms to have the coat put on. The aid moved to take the coat from Laura, but Laura shook her head.

"Let's let Rhia put on her own coat." Then she turned to Rhia. "I'm holding up your coat for you. Here are the armholes and the hood. Turn around and I'll help you."

Rhia stared at Laura again then sighed. She dropped her arms, turned around, and let Laura hold the coat up while Rhia slipped her arms through the sleeves. The aid watched with true amazement on her face. She said, "I didn't realize she could follow directions so well."

Laura and the aid talked about strategies to help Rhia do more for herself and how important that was for Rhia. It was fine to help when Rhia needed it, but it was also important to step back and let Rhia do as much for herself as possible.

Laura had intervened before Rhia could train her aid to become her maid. And Rhia knew it. She glanced at Laura and scowled, not even trying to pout. Rhia then took her aid's hand to go outside, ignoring Laura. Laura just smiled.

The girls in Rhia's class took Rhia under their wing and attempted to help her with everything. There were frequent fights about who got to sit with Rhia in the lunchroom or help

Rhia find a book. The teacher eventually assigned one person each day to be the primary helper, but there were arguments about that too. Everyone wanted to be Rhia's friend, even some of the boys. Two in particular argued over who got to push Rhia in her wheelchair on the playground. Rhia smiled at them like a princess watching two knights battle for a kiss.

Laura also came up with a way for Rhia to be included in PE. Rhia was connected to two girls, one on either side, who took her arms. The ball was brought closer and slowly rolled for Rhia to kick. After a few attempts, Rhia made contact and the ball went whizzing across the playing field. Rhia and her helpers ran together to first base, all three laughing as they tried to reach the base. Once the kids learned that having Rhia on your team was an automatic hit, they bickered over who got her on which team.

For the most part, Rhia has been blessed with great teachers. But sometimes a teacher believed Rhia needed to be pitied. Pity meant Rhia had to always be protected and not stressed too much. She wasn't required to work too hard or to get things for herself. If she bumped her elbow, she needed to be cuddled, and if she looked sad, she needed to be cheered up immediately. Rhia figured it out fast, and then played those people like a master con artist to get what she wanted. If she didn't want to get her own jacket, she just sighed like she was tired and her teacher or aid would run and get it for her. If a teacher said she needed to put the book down and return to her desk to work, Rhia's cute little lip would tremble as if she might cry, and then she'd get to stay where she was doing exactly what she wanted while everyone else in class had to work on spelling.

This strategy didn't work on every teacher. Occasionally an aid or a specialist would see Rhia just sitting at her desk waiting for someone to help her and would say, "Come on, Rhia. Get your hat. It's time to go outside." Then the aid would turn away, forcing Rhia to actually move and fetch an object for herself. In time, Rhia learned to run circles around the tougher teachers by enlisting the help of the kind teachers. If Rhia looked very, very sad the teachers who pitied her would defend Rhia's desire to be waited upon, and they'd argue with the teachers who expected her to do more for herself. While the teachers debated, Rhia continued to relax.

I wanted all of Rhia's teachers to demand more from Rhia. I didn't expect her to keep up with her classmates or complete all of her schoolwork, but I did expect her to say what she needed and do for herself what she could. I also secretly admired my daughter's ability to get what she wanted without lifting a finger. It was an excellent survival skill.

Lots of kids with disabilities learn to get people around them to do things they want. I don't see it as a negative; I see it as a smart way to get your needs met. The cuter you are, the easier it is to manipulate people. If you're not cute, just yell a lot. Teachers and aids will scramble to get you to be quiet.

This strategy doesn't work for every disabled child, though. I've watched dark-skinned disabled children crying exactly the same way their light-skinned disabled peers do, but their needs are ignored. Their communication style will be labeled as a "behavior." One day I saw a child with a face disfigurement that left them snotty and constantly drooling, sitting on the floor of their classroom, crying and asking for a hug, while another child, one who was cute and didn't drool, was hugged the moment she whimpered.

That cute child was mine.

Rhia is lucky. She is beautiful, blue-eyed, and white.

6

I EXPECTED RHIA TO DO HER BEST AND NOT USE HER disability to get out of doing work. Although some people looked at her with pity and let her get away with murder, some expected too much. This included her grandmother.

Laurent's mother was a highly educated psychologist who specialized in getting addicts of all types clean. Whether it was a drug, sex, or gambling addiction, her success rate was almost 100 percent. She charged top dollar, and her price was considered worth it. If you wanted to get clean, you went to Margorie. She also worked at the Haight Ashbury Clinic helping street junkies. A no-nonsense woman, she'd battled her own eating disorder and had zero tolerance for bullshit.

She adored Rhia, but when Rhia reached first grade, Margorie said she'd no longer read to Rhia until Rhia learned to read for herself. Margorie firmly believed that Laurent and I were coddling Rhia, and if we pushed her harder, Rhia would be forced to learn.

I wasn't there that day, but Laurent told me about their argument. He had brought Rhia over for a visit, and when Rhia held out a book to her Grandma Marg, her grandmother handed the book back and walked away. Later, Margorie told Laurent that Rhia could do more for herself than we believed and we should force her to learn to read. Laurent was furious with his mother, reminding her that Rhia was blind and delayed and couldn't read because she couldn't see the words, not because she was lazy. Margorie said Rhia wasn't lazy, she was manipulating her parents. They argued on and on while Rhia watched TV in the other room.

Margorie died in 2004, and I think about her sometimes, especially about her expectations of others. She was hard on herself and therefore hard on others, expecting the absolute best from people. She got results and saved many lives. She was passionate and dedicated, often funny, and she loved her family deeply. But sometimes her no-excuses attitude caused more harm than help. Rhia's disability wasn't something she could just battle by learning to read.

Sometimes when I watch Rhia determinedly walk down the hallway with her walker bashing the walls as she fights to keep moving forward, I see Margorie in her.

It's a difficult balance knowing when to give in to Rhia's complaints and when to make her keep trying. When Rhia got her foot orthotics at age seven, I made a huge mistake.

Rhia's body lacked proper muscle tone due to hypotonia. Therefore, the muscles that held her ligaments and bones in proper alignment didn't work. As she grew, Rhia's feet flattened and her ankles twisted, making walking even harder. She was prescribed articulated foot orthotics, otherwise known as AFOs.

We met the specialist who would create her AFOs in Santa Rosa, one hour south of Ukiah. He was a cheerful, patient man named Michael who knew exactly how to work with kids. While wrapping Rhia's feet, ankles, and calves in wet, gooey gauze, he kept her distracted by asking questions about *Rugrats*. Then while waiting for the gooey gauze to dry and harden, Rhia watched *Rugrats* videos. After forty minutes the "casts" had hardened, and Michael cut them off with a small buzzing saw that Rhia said tickled. Michael laughed with her, keeping her calm as he carefully removed each mold off her leg.

Two weeks later, we returned to Santa Rosa to try on Rhia's brand-new, perfectly molded, plastic AFOs. Michael showed me how to put them on and how to Velcro them so they stayed in place but weren't too tight. I had already bought a new pair of shoes one and a half sizes larger than Rhia's shoe size, just as Michael had instructed. Rhia had picked out sparkly purple tennis shoes with Velcro closures, and although she frowned when the AFOs were put on, she smiled when she looked at her new shoes. Then she stood to try walking in her new foot orthotics and cried.

"They hurt my feet!" she said, gripping my hand so hard I winced.

"Where does it hurt?" Michael asked.

Still gripping my hand, Rhia leaned over and pointed at the top of her foot.

Michael said, "Wear them for five minutes and then I'll check."

Rhia just stood there and refused to walk, but we still waited five minutes before he took them off. After checking her feet for red marks that indicated pressure or rubbing, he put them back on and said, "Walk to the car, and when you're in the car you take them off. Wear them a little every day until you get used to them."

Because Rhia liked him, she kept the AFOs on until she was strapped into the back seat of our car. Then she almost kicked me trying to pull off her new shoes.

Michael said to me, "Have her wear them for fifteen minutes a few times a day and look for any signs of redness. We don't want her to get a blister while she's adjusting to them. Eventually, she will wear them all day."

"Sounds like breaking in a new pair of hiking boots," I said.

He laughed. "It kind of is."

For the next month, Rhia and I battled over her AFOs. She kicked me in the chest or arms when I put them on her feet, and she often refused to stand or walk. When I eventually told her if she didn't wear them she would have to use her wheelchair all the time, she gave in. She watched me set the timer for fifteen minutes and then walked around the house holding my or Rick's hand, but the moment the timer went off she sat down and began ripping open the Velcro to get the AFOs off. I dutifully checked her feet afterwards and saw no tell-tale red marks. She appeared to be adjusting to them but still wasn't ready for all-day use. One day I decided to double the time she wore them and then took her out to run errands with me.

We walked into a gift shop, where she helped me look for a birthday gift. After ten minutes in the shop, she said her feet hurt. I encouraged her to walk to the bookstore on the next block, which was her favorite destination. She agreed, but when we were halfway there she began to whine loudly, "My feet hurt me."

I glanced at my watch. It had been twenty-five minutes. Surely she could wear them for a full thirty minutes! "Keep them on until we get into the store, then I'll carry you."

"Carry me now!" she cried, pulling her hand from mine and raising her arms.

"You can walk a little further, Rhia."

"No I can't! It hurts!"

I grabbed her hand, but she jerked it away. "Come on, Rhia. Five minutes. That's all. You have to wear them for five more minutes."

Rhia sat down on the sidewalk and crossed her arms, weeping.

I suddenly wanted to cry too as I fought my frustration. Why couldn't she understand I was trying to save her feet?! If she didn't use AFOs, she wouldn't be able to walk at all! Then what?

Taking a deep breath, I said, "Rhia, you are keeping those AFOs on for four minutes, whether you sit here or not."

Rhia kept crying, but she took my offered hand and stood. Then we finished our walk to the bookstore, where I sat her in a big, comfy chair and removed her AFOs.

On her right heel was a torn and bleeding one-inch blister. On her left heel, a two-inch red mark.

Scooping her into my arms, I sat on the chair with her in my lap and said, "Oh honey, I am so sorry."

She snuggled close and kept crying. My heart broke.

One of the women who worked in the shop asked if we were okay, and I said we just needed a minute. She gave me a box of tissues and smiled.

"Being a mom is hard sometimes," she said.

You have no idea, I thought.

It took several months for Rhia to tolerate her AFOs, but eventually she wore them all day, every day, for more than ten years. As she grew, Michael made a new pair from a new cast of her feet, and she got brand-new shoes and knee-high socks to go with them. We also called them "Rocket Boots" rather than AFOs. "Because they make me go faster," Rhia explained to Michael.

Some parents keep their baby's first pair of shoes. I kept Rhia's first AFOs. They are so small, barely big enough to cover her toes now. But they remind me of how tiny she used to be, how far she's come, and of the day I first learned the difference between when Rhia is fighting me just to get her way and when she's fighting me because there's something important she needs.

All these years later, it's still tricky to figure out which is which sometimes.

7

In the third grade, Rhia made a best friend, Anna. Anna was the opposite of Rhia but just as pretty, a tall, strong Latina girl with thick black hair. She instinctively knew how to talk to Rhia, and before long Anna was Rhia's primary "helper." Anna seemed to enjoy spending time with Rhia and would often seek her out on the playground or in class. No one told her to; Anna genuinely liked Rhia, and Rhia liked her as well. The two girls became fast friends, and in the fourth grade that friendship strengthened. A few other girls joined the clique, and soon Rhia was surrounded by real, honest friends. The kids loved being included in Rhia's O&M lessons; who wouldn't love getting out of class to buy ice cream with Rhia? In time, with the support of teachers (especially Laura) and the patience of four ten-year-old girls, Rhia learned how to be a friend in return. Rather than just expecting people to wait on her or do what she wanted, she learned that friendship is reciprocal. She gave compliments on Anna's new outfit or hairstyle. She shared her cookies with another girl at snack time. She gave away her crayons when another friend needed them.

There were six girls in her core social group who stayed together through grades three, four, and five: Kira, Jennifer,

Amber, Claire, Melissa, and, of course, Anna. All six were outgoing, upbeat, and smart. Kira and Amber loved horses and the outdoors, while Claire, Jennifer, and Melissa were more indoor types, preferring books and art. Anna was the shyest and also the only Latina. She tended to spend more one-to-one time with Rhia in class, while the other girls enjoyed hanging out with Rhia on the playground or during lunch. Rhia loved her crew of girls and looked for them as soon as she got off the bus. Several of the girls waited for her at their classroom door and then took turns walking with Rhia on the playground. When class started, Anna always sat with Rhia.

Despite the bond the girls shared, Rhia's grade-school friends behaved more like companions or caretakers. The girls took care of Rhia like she was much younger than they. And Rhia still spent far too much time surrounded by adults.

Perhaps the best indicator of elementary school social success is being invited to birthday parties. Not only was Rhia invited to several parties, but she also hosted three of her own, and everyone she invited came.

I went to every birthday party Rhia was invited to and tried to stay in the background as much as possible, making myself available for a trip to the bathroom or assistance with eating. I wanted Rhia to have an opportunity to just be a kid and hang out with her besties. Sometimes there were complications, like when there was a flight of stairs to climb to get up to a friend's bedroom. Whenever that happened, the parents hosting the event apologized, sounding embarrassed they hadn't thought of the problem ahead of time. I assured them it was not really an issue as I helped Rhia climb the stairs and then stayed within earshot so I could help her when the girls wanted to walk back down.

Once I intervened when three friends tried helping her down the stairs on their own.

"Thanks so much, girls, but I'll do it," I said. "She's a lot heavier than she looks, and she'll knock you down those stairs if she trips."

They laughed nervously as I picked up Rhia and carried her downstairs.

Rhia and her friends had a wonderful time at every party. However, the birthday girl's parents and I played an uncomfortable game called "Where does Mom fit in?" I was greeted warmly and offered something to drink, but then when the girls were off doing their own thing I was suddenly the extra mom in the room, standing in the corner of the kitchen with a plastic cup of root beer in my hand, trying to stay out of the way while the parents tried to make small talk. I'd offer to help, but they'd say they didn't need it. I'd move toward the doorway to check on Rhia and then look back at the parents and smile. They'd ask how Rhia was, and I'd say fine. There would be more silence as the parents bustled around the kitchen laying out napkins and plastic forks. I'd sip my root beer and watch. They'd smile at me and ask a question about the girls' school. Did Rhia like her teacher? Eventually the parents would stop busying themselves with party prep and would join me near the room where the girls were making some kind of birthday craft. That's when the parents would compliment me about how well I took care of Rhia and what a great mom I was and how wonderful Rhia was. I'd say something about how sweet their daughter was and what a great friend she was to Rhia.

It didn't matter which party or which parents; the questions were pretty much the same. I appreciated how hard they worked to include Rhia and make me feel welcome. The other parents dropped off their girls and drove away, returning in two or three hours to pick up their excited child just coming down from a sugar high. I couldn't do that and sitting in the car would have been weird, so I stood awkwardly in the kitchen waiting for Rhia to say she needed to use the bathroom.

I especially appreciated the moms who offered me a glass of wine instead of soda pop.

8

WHAT HAPPENS TO GIRLS BETWEEN FIFTH AND SIXTH grades? They leave school on the last day of fifth grade with big plans for their summer, waving and hugging their besties goodbye with the hope they'll see each other over break. And then they return for the first day of sixth grade, calmer, quieter, and aloof. Friendships end for mysterious reasons. Girls form new cliques, which can change weekly. You're in, then you're out, then you're in again, and often girls have no idea why. Learning how to survive the social pecking order of sixth grade girls seems to be a normal part of growing up. It can be painful to watch. Parents are utterly powerless when it comes to grade school bullying.

During the second month of the school year, Rhia's friend Kira ran up to me as I was leaving their classroom and informed me that Anna was no longer Rhia's friend.

"Anna called Rhia a retard and everyone laughed," she said, her face red with anger. Amber stood beside her and nodded.

I glanced through the window and saw Rhia taking her seat in class. She was smiling and chatting with her aid, who was helping her sit in her adapted chair safely. The aid had one hand on Rhia's back and the other holding the chair in place.

Another girl sitting at Rhia's table stared at her with a look on her face that screamed, "What's wrong with her?" Rhia looked at the girl and waved hello.

I turned back to Kira and Amber. "Thank you for telling me. I'll handle it. You two should get to class before you're late."

I think it was the adults' fault that Anna turned against Rhia. We put so much pressure on her to be Rhia's friend and helper that we didn't allow Anna to just be a kid. If Rhia's aid or teacher was out, the substitute would ask Anna what to do for Rhia. Anna was ten! Why did she become the number one Rhia expert at school? We all relied on this little girl too much, and that includes me. Of course she eventually rebelled.

Thankfully, Rhia seemed unaware of the teasing. She never complained about anyone being mean to her or about Anna's distance. Rhia was oblivious. The other girls in class were furious and came to Rhia's defense, creating a protective circle around Rhia as much as possible. They didn't just tell me, they told every teacher what was happening, and the bullies, including Anna, were punished.

Rhia couldn't imagine anyone being mean to someone, especially to her; bullying was a mystery Rhia couldn't conceive of. She was sad Anna wasn't her friend anymore, but she still had Amber, Kira, and the other three girls who called Rhia a friend. Rhia also didn't realize she was being bullied because she couldn't hear what Anna said. By the sixth grade, Rhia was almost deaf.

9

Tama, my Renaissance Faire friend, was horrified when she discovered that I had never taken my almost twelve-year-old daughter to Disneyland.

"It's an important part of everyone's childhood," she insisted.

"I can't afford it. And Rhia wouldn't like it."

"How do you know she wouldn't like it? She likes Disney movies."

"Yeah, but she doesn't like crowds and she'll hate going on rides. So why go?"

"I'm taking you two to Disneyland."

"Seriously, it's not that big a deal . . ."

"You are taking your daughter to Disneyland!"

There was no point arguing; if I didn't allow Tama to take Rhia and me to Disneyland I would never hear the end of it. Literally. Every time I'd see her until we were too old to talk, she would remind me how I never took my child to Disneyland.

It wasn't just the money and my belief that Rhia wouldn't like going. I didn't like Disneyland. The idea of surrounding myself with pastel painted flowers, princess parties, and people smiling like they had sunbeams pouring out of their asses made me cringe. Disneyland was for suckers who paid ridiculous sums of money to wear sparkly Mickey ears while watching parades on Disney Lane. It was not for intelligent, budget-conscious families.

Just before Rhia's thirteenth birthday in May 2008, Tama drove us the nine hours from her house in Tracy to Disneyland. Tama's daughter Cerri, who was five years younger than Rhia, joined us. We arrived at the Grand Californian Hotel on a hot Los Angeles evening, checked into our rooms, and then had Mickey Mouse–shaped pizzas for dinner in the hotel's restaurant. In the morning, we prepared to enter the Magic Kingdom. The two girls were the perfect princess companions in their sparkly gowns, Cerri in Princess Belle yellow and Rhia in light blue for Princess Cinderella. As we waited in line to enter the park, Cerri bounced beside Rhia's wheelchair, one hand resting on the handle as I pushed. Rhia giggled. As soon as we entered the gate, a woman said, "Welcome, princesses!" I wanted to say, "I'm not a princess." Both girls giggled more.

We strolled through one of the tunnels under the Disneyland train station and entered the Midwestern Americana fantasy small town of Main Street. That's when Rhia threw out her arms and sang as loud as she could.

As Rhia sang, Cerri bounced more and Tama laughed. I stared at my daughter in wonder as she sang with her arms held outward, as if she wanted to hug everyone in Disneyland.

"Don't worry if it's not good enough for anyone else to hear . . ."

People walking by smiled at her, and a few clapped their hands to show their approval. Tears filled my eyes and I just let them fall down my face. I had never seen Rhia so happy.

"Just sing . . . sing a song!"

I glanced at Tama, who was grinning at me.

"Shut up," I said, wiping my eyes.

"I didn't say anything," she said with a shrug, but "I told you so" was all over her face.

Before we could continue into Disneyland, we needed to check in at City Hall for Rhia's Disability Pass, a booklet that allowed her to sign up for a ride without having to stand in line. She would show her booklet to a "Cast Member" at one of the designated kiosks, and that person would stamp her card with the time she could go on a particular ride. It was like the FastPass system but without the restrictions.

Disneyland's disability services have gone through a lot of changes since 2008. One problem the company wanted to stop was non-disabled people paying disabled people to go to Disneyland with them so that everyone could cut to the front of lines. The Walt Disney Company considered this fraud, but I don't see it that way. Disneyland is extremely expensive, and most disabled adults are unemployed and live on Social Security. Why not hire yourself out for a trip to Disneyland for a day? It's simply another way disabled people survive and thrive in a world that excludes them.

The line at City Hall was long, and it felt sadly anticlimactic after Rhia's song. But once the person at Disability Services determined Rhia was indeed disabled and waiting in line would be a hardship, Rhia had her picture taken and the card issued. At last, we were free to play in Disneyland.

First stop was for the girls to get their hair done at the Bibbidi Bobbidi Boutique in Fantasyland. Rhia chose to have her long brown hair fixed into a simple bun like Cinderella. Cerri wanted long, flowing hair like Belle. Then we wandered around Fantasyland, exploring the castle, the drawbridge, Snow White's magic well, and the ducks in the moat. Tama and Cerri went on the Dumbo ride, but Rhia decided she didn't want to go. She wasn't interested in any of the rides; Rhia was waiting to meet her idol, Cinderella.

She first saw the movie *Cinderella* when she was a toddler. Over the years, Cinderella became Rhia's favorite character in the world. She likes the other movies, including my favorite, *Beauty and the Beast*, but Cinderella stirred Rhia's imagination more than any. She learned all the songs by heart, and even after she lost her hearing, she remembered the words. Rhia said that Cinderella was "a good friend to everyone and a good singer, like me." Cinderella was more than an imaginary friend; she was a role model for Rhia. And soon, she would meet her in real life.

Tama took us all to lunch at Ariel's Grotto, a princess-themed restaurant in California Adventure. To enter, Rhia had to take the elevator downstairs rather than the curving grand staircase. When the elevator doors opened and I wheeled Rhia forward, she gasped and said, "Ariel!" Standing about twenty feet from us was the real life Princess Ariel. Rhia didn't know she was an actress in a bright red wig and green dress, and even though I knew, I was excited too.

"Hello," Ariel said, her arms open wide. Cerri ran to her and hugged her tightly while I pushed Rhia in her wheelchair closer. Rhia reached up with both arms, and Ariel bent low to embrace her.

"What's your name?" Ariel asked.

"Rhia. I'm a princess too."

"You certainly are!" Ariel said. "Shall we take a picture together?"

Rhia unbuckled her seatbelt so I could help her stand for the picture. Ariel helped steady her, and the two girls in their beautiful gowns grinned with delight as the photographer took their photo.

I still have that photo.

After meeting Ariel, we were seated at our table and then ordered lunch. The ceiling of the room was painted blue-green like the sea, and around the gleaming golden chandeliers swam multicolored glass figures of starfish, jellyfish, and other sea creatures that seemed to be reflecting sunlight under the waves. Sparkling mermaids were painted on the walls, their tails embedded with seashells.

A trumpet sounded, and a man wearing a purple page's tunic and cap with a matching feather announced the princesses one by one. Each princess waved as she entered and then visited the children seated at the tables to sign autographs and pose for pictures. Cerri could barely sit still. Rhia sat quietly, holding her autograph book and smiling as she waited. Ariel . . . Aurora . . . Jasmine . . . and then at last, Cinderella. She was happy to see all the princesses and give each a hug, but Cinderella was Rhia's rockstar.

When Cinderella finally reached our table, Rhia stared with wide eyes and then leapt up, gripping the table to steady herself before I could help. Cinderella reached out to help as Rhia flung herself into Cinderella's arms. Cinderella laughed and hugged her tightly.

Rhia said, "I love you!"

Cinderella smiled and hugged her again. "It's so good to meet you."

I helped Rhia sit in her chair again so that Cinderella could sign both girls' autograph books. Afterwards, Cinderella kneeled by Rhia's chair and took her hand. She admired Rhia's dress, and then they compared the color to Cinderella's own gown.

Rhia told Cinderella how much she loved her. "You're super nice to everyone. I like that," she said.

"I can see that you're nice to everyone too. I believe you're a good friend."

Rhia giggled. "Yes."

When it was time for Cinderella to talk to the other children in the room, Rhia waved goodbye and then said loudly, "Cinderella is my friend."

Of course, I was crying again. Tama just grinned.

Tama grinned even more when Belle came to our table and I leapt up to have my picture taken with my favorite princess. Rhia shouted, "You're my mom's favorite!"

Belle just smiled as I grinned like a ten-year-old and Tama took the picture.

We have been to Disneyland every year since 2008. It is expensive, but since we don't spend money on after-school activities, extracurricular classes, or sports, it is easy to save for the trip. All the money that would have gone to uniforms or dancing lessons goes into the Disneyland pot, and once a year we spend it all, just so Rhia can have five minutes with Cinderella again.

Cinderella has also come to Rhia's birthday party twice. Every actress who portrays Cinderella gives Rhia the special attention she needs, as if they are channeling the compassion and kindness of the fantasy Cinderella. I know that Cinderella is considered a bad role model for young girls; she was rescued by a prince and fell in love after one dance! But now I see what Rhia sees. Cinderella was rescued by the animals she loved because through all the sadness and hardship of her childhood, she remained kind and compassionate. She is a friend to everyone, just like Rhia.

Disneyland really is the Magic Kingdom. It's the one place where Rhia is truly happy, and it's the one place in the world she belongs.

LOSS

"I have ataxia, but I'm still a princess.
I'm just a different kind of princess."

Rhia, age 14

1

I am often asked about Rhia's hearing. "What does she hear?" "Can she hear me at all?" "When did she lose her hearing?" "She looks like she hears me; are you sure she can't hear my voice?" "Why doesn't she wear hearing aids?" "Have you considered cochlear implants?"

The answers are:

- I don't know. I don't live in Rhia's skin and I don't have her ears.
- There is no way I can know what she does and doesn't hear. All I can do is guess, just as the doctors and the audiologist have guessed.
- We think she hears sound, but it's garbled, like trying to understand a foreign language under water.
- She doesn't hear high-pitched sounds. How do I know? Because when the smoke detectors go off she doesn't even flinch.
- She looks like she hears you because she used to be hearing so understands that you are speaking to her, and she is clever enough to make excellent guesses about what you are probably saying. But that too is

my guess. Maybe she can hear you sometimes, but it fades in and out.

- She tried hearing aids but hated them.
- A cochlear implant requires major surgery and she hates that too, so she learned sign language.
- Any other questions?

The questions are all about what she can and can't do. People listen to the answers, nod, attempt to communicate with her for about a minute, then move on. Once they have proven to themselves that Rhia can't hear, they stop trying to talk to her.

Occasionally I am asked, "How should I talk to her?" What a wonderful question! Instead of wanting to know how Rhia adapts, a person asks how they can adapt to her. I see people try to communicate with her and include her in an activity. It's not easy, and I don't blame people when they eventually give up. But the ones who really try to connect with Rhia are rewarded with her bright smile. If they know even a little sign language, Rhia beams and says, "They know my language!" All it takes is getting close, making sure she's looking at you, and then signing, "It's good to see you."

I know when people ask me about Rhia's hearing they aren't trying to be rude or cruel; they really want to understand and learn. And most of the time I don't mind answering. But after I'm asked a hard question, I wish they would follow up with a question about communication.

- "How does Rhia like to be included?"
- "What is her favorite thing to do?"

- "Can you help me sign a question?"
- "Does Rhia understand what is happening? How can I help her understand?"
- "Would Rhia like a cookie? How do I sign 'cookie'?"

The more people focus on who Rhia is and learn how to communicate with her, the more they discover she is a vibrant, funny, kindhearted girl who loves to sing and go for walks on sunny days. She's also deaf.

I first noticed Rhia was deaf when she was in the fifth grade and had surgery on her feet. For years she had worn the articulated foot orthotics, otherwise known as Rocket Boots, to support her hyperflexible joints and bones. Severely low muscle tone made her feet deform until she was walking on the inner sides of her feet. It was painful, so we chose an operation. She had both feet operated on at once to lessen the hospital trauma and spent four days in the hospital. While there, she complained she couldn't understand what anyone said and couldn't hear her music or the movies she watched. The doctors thought it was a side effect of the anesthesia and her hearing should improve in time. And it did, but not completely.

Two years after her surgery, Rhia's world probably sounded like whale calls in the ocean. And no one could figure out why or how her auditory processing ability had degenerated so quickly. The MRI didn't show any damage, and her ears appeared normal. But something was clearly wrong with the way her brain interpreted sound. Had the surgery damaged her hearing? And if it was damaged by anesthesia, wouldn't she have simply gone deaf instead of regaining her hearing, then slowly losing it again? It didn't make sense to me or her doctors.

Perhaps she was going deaf before surgery and the anesthesia just sped it up. Rhia is bright. She may have figured out how to read lips to understand what someone said before anyone knew she couldn't hear. Just get them close enough, concentrate on their mouth . . . voilà, instant understanding. Resilient and highly adaptable, Rhia fooled us all for a long time. Her mannerisms were those of a "hearing" person. Nod your head. Say yes. It took a while before we realized she didn't understand what we said.

"Do you want a cookie or an apple?" I'd ask.

"Yes."

"Which one? Cookie? Or apple?"

"I want it."

"But which one? A cookie . . ." I held up the cookie. "Or an apple?" I held up the apple. She stared at them and touched the one she wanted, tricking me into believing she needed a visual cue to make a choice rather than not understanding the words I spoke.

Smart girl.

It was unfair! She was already blind, and her hand tremors were so bad she couldn't use braille, so she needed her hearing to learn and communicate. Her schoolbooks were on tape and she had excellent recall. Now that too was being taken from her.

By the time Rhia was eleven, she'd been to a lot of doctors and had hundreds of tests, but the one she hated the most was audiology. She liked the doctor fine, but the tedium of the tests and being told that she needed hearing aids depressed her more than any blood draws could.

"No! I don't need them," she insisted, even after the hearing test showed she couldn't hear voices. Dutifully she put the block in the box when she heard the tone, but she also put a block in after guessing the interval between testing tones. The doctor mixed up the timing to avoid that, so it was obvious when Rhia was guessing. And during the vocabulary test she got frustrated when she couldn't identify what any of the words were. I made sure she could see the pictures, and she identified them by looking, but when asked to point to the "baseball" or "ice cream," she just looked at me and said, "I can't find it."

After the test, the doctor pressed cold putty into Rhia's left ear to make an impression to create a mold for new hearing aids. That's when Rhia cried and flung out her fist to hit the doctor.

"No!" Rhia screamed. "I don't want them!!!"

I held Rhia close to my chest and soothed her the best I could while she sobbed. The audiologist quickly made impressions of each ear and then left the room.

I wiped Rhia's face with a tissue and then wiped away the pink residue of the putty that clung to the small hairs in Rhia's ears.

Rhia asked, "Why can't I hear no more? It doesn't make sense."

"I don't know, baby," I said and hugged her again.

We both cried during the three-hour drive home.

Sensorineural hearing loss: the ears hear but the brain doesn't understand the sounds. The cause is still unknown.

For two long years, Rick and I insisted that Rhia wear hearing aids, even when her ears became so irritated she got eczema. Rhia would wear them for a few hours at a time before she'd rip them from her red and itching ears. I would dutifully rub cortisone cream into the skin of each ear and then plop the hearing aids back in for another hour. We kept trying because we hoped she'd get used to them and then wouldn't be so isolated from her hearing friends and family. But I wonder if they helped at all. Rhia's ears actually worked, but her brain couldn't figure out what she was hearing. The hearing aids amplified sound but couldn't make sound clear. I suspect that amplification only made the confusion of noise that Rhia lived with louder.

Because Rhia was clinically deaf, a new teacher was added to Rhia's IEP team in the sixth grade. Julie, teacher of the deaf and hard of hearing, was assigned to teach Rhia American Sign Language (ASL). Julie was vibrant and talkative, with long black hair and a quick smile. Rhia liked her immediately, which made learning ASL easier. Just like when Rhia tried to learn braille, her ataxia impeded her ability to make ASL signs, so she continued to use her voice. But her vision was strong enough to see and understand when other people signed to her.

Sadly, Rhia lost the ability to communicate with her small band of friends, which was worse than losing her hearing. My sociable and cheerful daughter grew quieter and more alone as her friends stopped trying to talk to her. She was learning the skills she needed to communicate, but she laughed less. When she started middle school the following year, Rhia's childhood friends were gone.

Rhia entered middle school officially deaf-blind. I longed for Rhia to go back to being that feisty, funny, joyful child she once was. As her isolation grew, I became more determined to help her. I signed up for an ASL class at the community college and learned more about deaf-blind communication.

2

MIDDLE SCHOOL IS A DIFFICULT TRANSITION FOR EVERY child, but for Rhia, I think it must have felt incomprehensible. One day she was surrounded by friends in her cheerful classroom, and the next she was on a completely different campus across town and all her friends had vanished into different rooms. Some of those rooms were on the second floor, which made it impossible for her to follow them if she wanted. Her new classroom was in the back of the school again, a place none of her friends visited. Even her lunch schedule was separate from theirs. At the same time, her body was changing like all of her friends, but Rhia couldn't comprehend why. She couldn't talk to anyone about what she was going through because she could barely hear her own voice, let alone someone else's. The only one who really understood her was me, her mom, but what thirteen-year-old girl wants to confide in their mother?

I remembered how awful my seventh grade experience was, and I wanted to cry when I thought of how much more Rhia had to endure. I had been bullied too, but Rhia was abandoned.

Angry is not a strong enough word to describe how I felt during Rhia's middle school years. Everything Rick and I had fought for dissolved when Rhia entered seventh grade. We had sold our house and moved to a new city so she could have friends and be fully included in her school. We had collaborated with her teachers and supported all the homework, lessons, and therapies her education team recommended. Rhia entered the Science Fair because all of the other sixth graders were doing it, so she could have that experience. She wanted to do a project about garbage, so we created a display showing how much trash was created if everyone in her school dropped one piece of paper. I put in extra hours on some of the work she couldn't do, but when all of Rhia's friends stopped by her presentation and told her how much they liked it, it was worth it. I wanted Rhia to belong, and for four lovely years she belonged at Oak Manor. Then, simply because she aged a year, Oak Manor was taken away and in its place was Pomolita Middle School. Once again, she was stuck in a classroom in the back of the school and reminded she didn't belong with "normal" students.

I fought for inclusion again and her teachers were willing to try, but I quickly realized the middle school model of moving from classroom to classroom made inclusion impossible for Rhia. She didn't have the stamina or sensory ability to change rooms five times a day. After one week full of logistical problems (which class required the bulky closed-circuit television system the most?) and an exhausted Rhia, the plan was abandoned. Next, I requested that we try having Rhia attend one art class with her friends. The art teacher set up a table in her room to accommodate Rhia's wheelchair, but after two weeks Rhia said she didn't want to go to art class anymore.

"Why don't you want to go?" I asked. She just shrugged and looked away.

The next day when I dropped Rhia off at school, her aid took me aside and explained. "The other girls ignore Rhia. Even the ones she was friends with. I think it makes Rhia sad."

Art class was canceled on that day, and I was forced to accept that Rhia would spend the next two years in the special education classroom. Ever the problem solver, I sat in my car and thought of how I could let those girls know they had hurt Rhia and make them feel bad and weren't they ashamed and... Then I thought I would sue the school for having a two-story building without an elevator. That was a lawsuit just waiting to happen! Who builds an inaccessible school?

There was nothing I could do to change a damn thing, so instead I sat in my car and cried for my daughter and for all she had lost.

Raising a disabled child is a frustrating dance, even though the steps are simple. One step forward, two steps back. Five steps forward, four steps back. You move forward for a few steps, then you have to step backwards several more. It's always a straight line back and forth, but the number of steps forward and back keeps changing. Sometimes you'll step back so much that you're behind the place you originally started. Occasionally you'll step forward and back until you realize you keep landing in the exact same spot. If you're lucky, you'll move forward a couple of steps before stepping back, so that over time, foot by foot, you slowly move ahead. The dance goes on and on until your child is all grown up and out of school.

Middle school felt more like a mosh-pit than an organized dance.

3

There is an anger that builds so slowly you don't recognize it as rage. It starts as irritation at the bank when there aren't enough tellers open for the line of eight people you're standing in. Yes, it's a perfectly normal feeling to have. The same for the irritation at the grocery store when an old lady leaves her cart in the middle of the aisle as you're trying to get past. Again, a completely ordinary feeling triggered by a completely normal daily occurrence. You take a deep breath, roll your eyes, then politely say excuse me as you squeeze your cart past hers. Irritation may feel like your skin is too dry and tight. That irritation grows into impatience, which makes it impossible to hold still. Red stoplights feel longer, and everyone around you seems to slow down. You take the dog for a walk and every time the dog stops to sniff yet another bit of grass near the sidewalk you jerk her collar, saying, "Come on!" Your dog happily keeps moving until the next clump of grass. Again you want to yank her collar to keep her moving.

You're under a lot of stress, so the irritation and impatience feel perfectly acceptable. But before you know it, the sensations grow into aggravation and the feeling that you're clenching your teeth to keep from yelling. Your jaw aches, your hands shake, and your heart pounds. You blame it on too much coffee and assume giving up caffeine will help.

But if you stop trying to explain the sensations with your mind and simply allow your body to feel them, you will discover a tight ball of tension in the center of your being that swirls like a tornado pressing against your ribs. It will frighten you because you're convinced that if you let it out, you'll burn down your neighborhood with its ferocity.

One morning in January we ran out of decaf, and even though I knew I should stay away from caffeine, the smell of a freshly brewed pot of coffee at 5:30 a.m. was too strong to resist.

"You know that's caffeine," Rick said.

I nodded and poured myself a cup. "A little won't hurt me." I gulped it down with a shot of peppermint-chocolate soy milk, feeling my taste-buds shout to my brain, *Wake up!* Then I began the task of getting Rhia ready for school.

Can someone please explain to me why Rhia's middle school thought starting school at 7:20 a.m. was a good idea, especially since the bus came by 7:00, which meant we had to get up at 5:30 to get ready in time?

Rhia was her usual sleepy self, eating her breakfast with half-closed eyes, brushing her teeth, and then getting dressed with some assistance from me. I raced around preparing her school snack, cleaning her glasses and hearing aids, finding her shoes, all while noshing on a piece of toast.

At 7:00, the battery cover of her left hearing aid fell off completely. It had been broken for a while and only stayed on through careful balancing of the hinge and scotch tape. After taping it back together and popping it into Rhia's ear, I began shoving her fingers into bright red gloves. The low muscle tone in her hands made her fingers bend and twist, so each finger had to be carefully maneuvered into the glove.

"Mommy, we have to put my coat on first," Rhia said, just as the bus pulled up in front of our house.

I shook my head and said, "No, we don't. Hold still. The bus is here." Yanking the sleeve of her raincoat, I fought to pull her gloved hand through.

Rhia jerked her hand out of her sleeve. "It won't work."

"Hold still!" I snapped. Then I jerked the jacket off, pulled off her gloves, shoved her jacket back on, and yelled at her gloves as I forced her fingers into them. "Why does this have to be so fucking hard?"

Rhia stared at me with wide eyes, her lips pressed tightly together.

Once she was bundled up, I took a deep breath and calmly said, "Come on. The bus is waiting."

Taking her arm, I pulled the walker toward her, then practically dragged her and the walker out the door. The dog blocked our way, eager to dash outside and say hello to the bus driver.

"Get out of the way!" I shouted. The dog just froze. As soon as Rhia had ahold of the door frame I jerked the walker away and swung it toward the dog. "I said get the hell out of the way!" The dog ducked.

Whoa . . . what am I doing? I took a deep breath, carried the walker down the steps, then turned to help Rhia out of the house and onto the bus. After buckling her into her seat I kissed her forehead and said, "Have a good day."

She just looked at me with big eyes.

The dog stayed out of my way as I walked into the house. Before I shut the door I said, "Come here, Boo." The dog reluctantly came closer. I leaned down and stroked her head. "Good girl." The dog forgave me immediately, of course, but I wondered if Rhia would.

Irritation. Impatience. Aggravation . . . anger. There was no room in my life for anger. I needed to be calm and tenacious. Schools and therapists don't listen to angry parents. Angry parents are labeled irrational. Angry parents get thrown out of meetings and important people's offices. Angry parents are ineffective at getting what their child needs.

If your child has a disability, it is vital that you remain in control at all times. Don't show emotion. Stay organized. Keep meticulous files. Return phone calls promptly. Remain polite but firm. And shove all of that anger and fear deep down into a tight ball, until the pressure in your core is so strong you're afraid you might crack a rib if you stay silent one more day.

I took my dog for a walk and tried to breathe every time she sniffed a clump of grass. My thoughts battered me with shame.

You've got to get control of yourself.

I'm trying.

You're doing a crappy job.

Gee, that's helpful!

The conversation in my head bounced back and forth between criticism and pleading.

What are you so angry about anyway?

Rhia. I'm angry about Rhia.

You're mad at Rhia?

Of course not! I'm mad at everything around Rhia. Her school and her hearing and her friends! I'm mad at everything she's lost, and no matter how hard I work I can't make it better!

Okay . . . makes sense . . . So what can you do?

I don't know!

I must have jerked the dog's leash because she stopped and dropped her head like she was in trouble. Reaching down to scratch her head, I said, "Good dog, Boo." She wagged her tail and we continued walking.

What can I do to make anything better?

When Rhia came home from school that day, I kneeled in front of her so she could clearly see my face and said, "I'm sorry I got so grumpy this morning. I was mad at the hearing aids and got frustrated. I shouldn't have yelled at you. It wasn't your fault."

She smiled and hugged me. "That's okay, Mommy. I get frustrated too sometimes."

It took several weeks and more conversations in my head while walking the dog before I knew what to do. I had to focus on what was, not what I wanted to happen. I admit, I've never been very good at this. I had studied meditation and Buddhism for ten years by the time Rhia reached middle school, and it was obvious from the rage I was feeling about her new school that I hadn't learned a damn thing about acceptance.

I focused on Rhia's new teacher, Mrs. Holden. She was a gray-haired woman in her late forties who liked wearing flower print dresses and gold hoop earrings. If she didn't smoke, then I was sure she once had because of the firm lines around her mouth and her scratchy, heavy voice. She'd been a special education teacher for twenty-five years, but unlike many teachers with that much experience, she was open to new ideas. Rhia was a challenge, and this teacher was ready. She opened her door to Laura and me and accepted every suggestion we threw at her. If it didn't work, she didn't worry about it; she just asked for the next idea. Mrs. Holden may have been stuck in the back of the school in a dark, older classroom with poor ventilation, but her imagination and flexibility shone bright. Plus, Rhia liked her.

Rhia in middle school was when I understood there were limits to my problem-solving powers. Up until then, I believed that Rhia's disabilities were a problem to be figured out. I knew I couldn't cure her disabilities, but I thought that I could smooth the way so nothing would impede her happiness. If I was smart enough and stayed tenacious, every obstacle could be obliterated.

I was wrong.

4

WITHOUT CAREGIVERS, PEOPLE WITH DISABILITIES AND the people who love them are screwed. I am my daughter's caregiver, but I rely on other caregivers to help me. I need to work to keep food on the table and a roof over our heads. Without other trusted caregivers, my little family would be living in our car. Rick has always worked, but it's nearly impossible to survive on one paycheck, especially in California. I also need other caregivers to give me a break when I'm worn out; providing 24/7 care is impossible for even the most dedicated parent. We need someone we can trust to share the load.

Caregivers also provide greater autonomy for the person with disabilities. Rhia has learned greater independence by having other people than her mom care for her. She has learned to trust others and express her needs, while also standing up for herself when she doesn't like something. No teenager or adult should be completely dependent on their mom for everything. Rhia has developed relationships with others who technically work for her. She has also learned to treat other people with respect while advocating for her own needs. Caregivers are her friends.

Unfortunately, caregivers make very little money for such a tough job, which means most caregivers can't afford to stay in the profession. An experienced caregiver is worth far more than the slightly above minimum wage they are paid. The job is both physically and mentally demanding. They care for the disabled person's body by supporting toileting, hygiene, and food intake. They also care for the person's mental well-being and emotional health. Caregivers are often required to manage behavioral and mental-health challenges, while also remaining respectful of the disabled person's own choices. Often they must learn the disabled person's unique communication style. All of Rhia's caregivers learned beginning ASL at the basic communication level. Caregivers also attend doctor's appointments with the disabled person; Rolina, one of Rhia's caregivers, came to every Stanford appointment with us, three hours' drive each way. She focused on Rhia while I focused on the doctor, making appointments less stressful for everyone.

For such a demanding job, why are caregivers paid so little? Most caregivers are paid through government agencies, like In Home Support Services and the Regional Center in California. Or they are paid through a nonprofit. Both of these types of payers have limits on what they can pay, limits set either by the government or by their grants. There are some caregivers who are paid by the disabled person or the disabled person's family, but very few people can afford to pay out of pocket the real value of a caregiver.

A skilled, experienced caregiver is vital to the quality of life of a disabled person. Without caregivers, too many disabled adults are forced to live with family or in an institution. They are unable to live autonomous lives or keep a job. How many intelligent and ambitious disabled adults are unemployed and forced to live with their grandparents? Too many.

Rhia had several caregivers who came to the house after school and on weekends so I could work or just take a break, and I am grateful for them all. The Regional Center paid for Rhia's caregivers through either a direct-support agency, a program that provided daily help, or a respite agency, a program that gave breaks to the family. Reflecting on the choice I made allowing Rhia to take an intelligence test I knew she'd fail, I was grateful I had.

The caregivers were all women, aged between early twenties and mid-forties. Some would work for a few months, but occasionally we'd get a caregiver who stayed for many years. Those women were the caregivers who eventually became part of our family.

Choosing a caregiver wasn't easy. The agency sent a candidate to the house to meet Rhia, and I would decide if they were a good option based on how well they interacted with Rhia and how much she liked them. After I talked to the candidate about Rhia's needs, I led them to Rhia's bedroom to meet her. While I stood near the door in case they needed help with communication, Rhia cheerfully chatted with the person and showed them her doll collection. If the candidate warmed up to Rhia and remained engaged with her, I gave that person a good mark. If they also tried communicating directly with her, I gave them another good mark. But ultimately the choice was Rhia's. I watched her while she showed off her toys and large book collection. Sometimes Rhia didn't ask the person to read a book to her, which meant Rhia wasn't sure about them. If she didn't talk to them directly and instead relied on me to communicate, I knew Rhia didn't like them. I wasn't always sure why Rhia didn't warm up to a potential caregiver, but if she stayed quiet or turned her back on the person, I didn't hire them, no matter how much I liked that person.

There have been four caregivers that Rhia liked immediately, and of those, three stayed in her life for many years. People who choose caregiving as a profession are the warmest, strongest, and most patient people on the planet. They can make a lot more money working as a cashier at Walmart, but they choose to work for people with disabilities. They want meaningful work that directly helps others.

Molly started working with Rhia when Rhia entered high school. Molly was a single mom in her forties with two teenage kids a little older than Rhia. With her thick blond curls, multiple tattoos, and rock band T-shirts tucked into faded jeans, she fully embodied her now sober, rocker-chick self. She'd been through a lot in her life but had gotten through it with her kindness and compassion still intact. She called Rhia "Sugar." Sadly, after a year and a half she could no longer live on the wage she got from the agency, so she moved back to her home state of New York. Thanks to social media, we've stayed in touch, and I'm happy to see she is thriving today. She still writes, "Hi Sugar," whenever she sends a note to Rhia.

Lindsey was nineteen and only a year older than Rhia when she began working for us. She too had been through a lot in her short years, but she kept her sense of humor and empathy. She and Rhia bonded as tight as sisters. Lindsey had the energy and imagination to try new things and test Rhia's limits. She took Rhia on long walks in the wheelchair around town, exploring unknown streets in Ukiah. The two girls went window shopping and got snacks at the local cafe, chatting with friends and strangers alike. At home Lindsey organized art projects for the two to do together. I still have several Christmas ornaments they made that look like cupcakes, made out of glass balls, paper cupcake holders, paint, and glitter.

We took Lindsey with us to Disneyland one year. It was her first time. She pushed Rhia's wheelchair for miles! I will never forget the look on her face when we met the Fairy Godmother near Snow White's wishing well. She was twenty years old and trembling with excitement while still trying to look cool when I took their picture.

Lindsey had dreams of moving to San Francisco, so when a friend who lived there asked me if I knew anyone who would make a good live-in nanny, I recommended Lindsey. It was hard to let her go. Everyone was tearful on her last day, but she was so excited to live in the big city. She couldn't spend the rest of her life taking care of Rhia. We have stayed in touch over the years, again through social media and occasional phone calls. Today she is almost thirty and has a daughter of her own.

Before Lindsey left, Rolina arrived. She was five months pregnant and I assumed she'd leave before the baby was born, but Rhia liked her, and I needed someone to replace Lindsey. Instead of leaving, she remained Rhia's caregiver for five years.

Rolina had long black hair and olive skin. Outgoing and cheerful, she too had nonstop energy. She was also strong. She could pick up Rhia with one arm while holding her newborn in the other. She pushed Rhia's wheelchair all over town while carrying her baby on her back. Because Rhia loved babies so much I let Rolina bring her daughter to work with her, even though it was against the agency's rules. Two years later Rolina had a little boy, and both of her children spent the day crawling or toddling around my house.

Rhia both loved having the babies in her house and hated how they made such a huge mess of everything. Somehow, Rolina managed to keep up with a toddler who loved to climb, a baby who put everything in his mouth, and Rhia who needed extra help. I often came home from work to the sound of a crying baby and the floor of my house covered in toys and clothes. Rolina would be busy giving Rhia and the toddler a snack while trying to do my dishes. I'd scoop up the baby and snuggle him until he fell asleep, while Rolina finished the dishes and cleaned up the kid mess. She and I would share gossip about the town and complain about our spouses like old friends. Over the years, Rolina's kids bonded with me as much as Rhia bonded with them, and I soon became "second mom." I loved holding Rolina's baby boy and rocking him to sleep while her daughter showed me all of Rhia's dolls she'd dragged from Rhia's room. Rhia allowed it, as long as Rolina put everything back where it was.

When Rolina's daughter turned four they came with us to Disneyland. It was the perfect age for a little girl to meet the princesses, and Rhia loved playing big sister. Rolina's spouse came too, a tall quiet man who tended to be shy but was kind and laughed often with Rhia. It felt like going to Disneyland with a family, complete with a crying two-year-old. When Rolina and her husband took their daughter on a ride, Rhia held their son on her lap while I pushed them both in the wheelchair.

"I'm like a big sister," she said with a grin.

The only reason Rolina stopped being Rhia's caregiver was the pay. Rent and food keep going up, but a caregiver's pay is limited to what the state will pay. To take care of her children's needs as they entered elementary school, she took a job at a bank that paid double what she earned as a caregiver. But our relationship has stayed strong. Rolina and her little family are as important to me as my brother and his family. We still see each other as often as we can and have remained close friends. I am still "second mom" to both of her kids.

In 2015, caregivers in California went on strike to demand overtime pay because under federal labor rules, caregivers were exempt from overtime pay and sick leave. Since most caregivers worked ten to twelve hours a day, they were missing out on significant hourly pay. But rather than raising awareness of the importance of caregivers, the strike pitted caregivers against the disabled community. Disabled people protested against caregivers' demands out of fear they would be unable to pay overtime and therefore lose their personal caregivers. If that happened, they would be forced to move into institutions. While the battle over changing the labor rules was fought, some caregivers were forced to walk out on the people they cared for, which was devastating for both the caregiver and the disabled person. I was heartbroken watching the two sides fight each other because the argument between caregivers and the people they cared for was misguided. The two sides should have banded together and focused on the real problem: government funding. By pitting the two sides against each other, the government wasn't held accountable for its lack of proper funding for services that supported disabled people.

Because I was a family caregiver, I was out of the argument. I had joined the union because I believe in the power of united workers fighting for their rights, but I would be Rhia's caregiver for the rest of her life whether or not I was paid or how many hours I worked. But I did attend union meetings and talked about how the government was turning caregivers into scapegoats. Members nodded in agreement, but there was no action to try to get the disabled community to stand with the caregivers. I also wrote about the issue on my caregiving blog as a way to reach the disabled community.

> People with disabilities are concerned that they will lose caregiver hours because agencies will stop paying the full hours people need to stay in their homes. Private pay employers won't be able to afford their workers. Caregivers are angry because they are paid low wages but must work more than eight hours a day. Caregivers are fighting for a livable wage and people with disabilities are fighting to live.
>
> It's time for caregivers and people with disabilities to stop fighting each other. People need to stay in their homes and workers need a livable wage. Rather than suing each other, it is time for both groups to unite and demand increased funding for programs that support the disabled. We need to examine our society and ask why we are so willing to throw people away simply because they can't care for themselves.

This battle over wages reflects a deeper problem. People with disabilities are not considered viable members of society and therefore have no value. The people who care for them are primarily people of color and women, groups traditionally considered low status. The system of caring for people with disabilities is structured around "cost savings." As long as it is shown that keeping people in their homes saves society money, then doing so is considered important.

Caregivers work as nurses, housekeepers, drivers, secretaries, and cooks. They often bathe, dress, and help toilet severely disabled people and are paid minimum wage. Despite the long hours, most caregivers are dedicated to their clients and feel that they are making a difference in the world.

People with disabilities rely on their caregivers to not only support their physical needs but also to help them engage with the world and enjoy their lives. The threat that a disabled person may lose their support if a pay increase is mandated is real. State budgets are strapped and agencies are run with minimal staff. And for those who have to pay out of pocket for caregivers, the changes could force them to go into an institution simply because their insurance will pay for it.

Rhia had zero understanding of the argument. Rolina didn't work overtime and wasn't in the union so she didn't go on strike. Eventually caregivers did receive overtime pay, but just as the disabled community feared, getting a quality caregiver became harder and more expensive. I suspect many family members had to step in to fill the gap that increased wages created.

I am my daughter's caregiver. I also rely on other caregivers to help me keep my daughter in our home. I gladly work far more hours than I am paid, and I know caregivers who do the same. Many of these workers are not family members, but they know that if they didn't donate hours their clients would suffer. I am grateful for their help.

5

Do you remember what it was like to be fourteen? Whatever your gender, I suspect you felt awkward in your constantly changing body. You'd finally get a handle on the changes, and then more hormones would transform you back into a gawky creature with greasy hair. Pimples and mood swings dominated your life. Every feeling was heightened, and every moment became epic.

Now imagine having to cope with all of that while also going deaf.

Rhia was fourteen when she walked into my room one day and announced, "I don't wear my glasses no more."

I recognized the battle in the way she stood, her arms stiff and hands gripping her walker. Her eyes stared directly into mine.

"You don't?" I needed to listen before telling her she had to wear her glasses.

"Nope. They don't help me so I don't know why I gotta wear them."

"Because your teacher asked you to. She says they seem to help when you're working on your computer."

"Well, they don't. So I'm not gonna wear them anymore." Before I could formulate a response that would encourage her to wear them while reminding her that she needs to do what her teacher tells her, she moved on to a new topic. "And my hearing aids don't do nothing either, so I don't know why I gotta wear them."

Pick your battles, I thought. At that stage in the game, the hearing aids were more important.

"Your hearing aids do help. You seem able to hear me better with them on."

"No they don't. They just bug me."

"I'm sorry about that, sweetie. We'll go to the audiologist again and she can fix them for you."

Rhia shrugged. "It don't matter. I don't need to wear them. And I don't know why nobody can do nothing about my ataxia." Her voice grew loud with frustration. "I hate my ataxia and nobody can fix me."

Taking a deep breath while biting my lip, I said, "I know. It's really frustrating."

"Yeah." She leaned over her walker and shouted, "I wish somebody could make my ataxia just go away!"

I stepped closer and wrapped my arms around her, feeling her whole body trembling as she let go of her walker to cling to me.

She said, "It's what I wish for. But I guess some wishes are too big and can never come true."

Don't cry, I thought. What the hell could I say? Everything she said was true. Her glasses only helped a little, her hearing aids barely helped at all, and her ataxia was worse every year. She used to be able to walk short distances without using a walker, but by age fourteen she had to use the walker constantly, even in the house.

Rhia was burned out, frustrated, and depressed. Nothing had helped, not the surgery on her feet, the new knee braces, the ongoing exercises, the eyeglasses or the hearing aids, not the super amino acids, and not the walker. The stubborn gleam in her eye that once embraced each new challenge with excitement was gone. She had once believed she'd get stronger if she did twenty sit-ups every day. By the eighth grade, she understood five sit-ups didn't matter.

When you realize that all your efforts won't change anything, how do you keep moving forward? Even an adult would feel despondent, so how was a fourteen-year-old child supposed to cope? And what could any mother do?

There were very few blind students in all of California in 2008, and of those, there were even fewer deaf-blind students. Individual school districts hired specialists to educate blind students, but it was financially impossible to hire a competent specialist to educate just one or two deaf-blind kids. The State of California funded a program called Deaf-Blind Services. Only two experts on educating deaf-blind students traveled throughout California, providing technical assistance and educational planning. They didn't do the teaching themselves; instead, they trained the teachers and specialists who worked with deaf-blind kids. Because every kid is unique, including deaf-blind kids, the first thing the expert did was observe the student in school. Then they would provide an in-depth report with recommendations on what each individual student needed at school.

Laura happened to know one of the experts who worked for Deaf-Blind Services, a Welshman named David Brown. He was intrigued before he met Rhia. "Rhiannon" is a common name in Wales, but David had never met a child outside his homeland with that name. When he met Rhia in person, he was even more intrigued.

Rhia was polite and smiled warmly but remained distant; she had developed a typical thirteen-year-old's reserve that required new people to work hard for her acceptance. David understood. He sat in the back of the room and observed Rhia working on lessons. He watched her eat her lunch with help from an aid, and then observed her interacting with teachers and classmates. He paid close attention to how she communicated her needs to others, including me.

Within the first hour it was clear to David that Rhia missed the majority of what was happening during her day. She missed seeing a classmate wave his arm and yell Rhia's name to get her attention from across the table. She didn't notice what the teacher was doing when the teacher talked to the entire class rather than directly to Rhia. And several times during her school day Rhia's whole body slumped and she stared off into space, unable to concentrate or even see what was in front of her. It clearly took an incredible amount of energy for Rhia to use her functional vision, decipher the scramble of sounds she picked up, concentrate on the simple signs and pictures her aid used to help her decipher those sounds, and try to get any schoolwork or actual learning accomplished.

David also saw that after Rhia ate a small snack she grew more cheerful and communicative. But an hour later, she drooped like a thirsty flower. Her teachers and I hadn't noticed the regular ebb and flow of Rhia's energy, and of course I beat myself up for missing it; mom guilt is a powerful enemy.

When I think about it now, David may have been the first person to recognize the signs of mitochondrial disease.

Besides providing Rhia frequent snack breaks, David recommended that Rhia's teacher use a microphone when she was talking to the class and that the speaker be on Rhia's worktable. That way, Rhia would know that her teacher was speaking and she could then focus her attention on her teacher. Although her teacher was uncomfortable about using a microphone, she again surprised me by her willingness to try it. And it worked. Rhia didn't always understand what her teacher said, but she paid attention when her teacher talked, which helped Rhia grasp a little bit more of the lesson.

The biggest recommendation from David was that Rhia have her own dedicated aid who was a trained intervener. An intervener is an interpreter for a person who is deaf-blind, but they don't just use ASL to interpret the words someone is speaking. They interpret the whole environment the deaf-blind person is in. An intervener signs what the teacher says, while also supporting the use of technology to access the curriculum and at the same time pointing out the student's friend saying hello.

An intervener training program was in development by the California Deaf-Blind Services in collaboration with San Francisco State University but wasn't operating yet. The official program would open three years later. Rhia would be a test of the program, a way to try out the curriculum as it was being developed.

After an extra IEP meeting, during which David's report was presented and both Laura and I advocated, the district agreed to hire an intervener with training being provided by Deaf-Blind Services. Laura agreed to be the intervener's supervisor. The district transferred a woman from a different school who was interested in the extra training required to be an intervener. Her name was Lois. Happily, Rhia liked her. Not only was Lois good at supporting Rhia academically, but she became an integral part in helping Rhia make new friends.

6

A GIRL WITH DOWN SYNDROME NAMED TANYA WAS A year younger than Rhia. She hadn't been in the same classes with Rhia at Oak Manor, so they didn't meet until they started at Pomolita. Once Rhia realized that Tanya was following her around as a way to say hi, Rhia and she became close friends. Tanya didn't speak, but she pointed to objects and pictures, which Rhia understood. Rhia used her voice, and Tanya had no problem understanding Rhia's often shaky spoken language. They sat together during class and ate their lunch together side by side at the large wooden table under the awning near the special education classroom door. Tanya was strong, so she could push Rhia's wheelchair anywhere she wanted to go. Tanya was outgoing, while Rhia was shy. Tanya was brave, while Rhia remained cautious. They were a perfect team.

Tanya's brother Albert, who also had Down syndrome, was the same age as Rhia. He was one of the boys who had liked to push Rhia's wheelchair at Oak Manor during recess, but at Pomolita he had to take turns with his sister. Eventually two other classmates, both girls, began following Rhia, Albert, and Tanya as they walked on campus, creating a small team of explorers. Rhia directed the exploration and everyone did what she said, with Tanya or her brother taking turns pushing her chair.

I watched them one day, this band of five special education students who braved the stares and giggles of the regular middle schoolers. One girl Rhia knew from Oak Manor said hello but then quickly moved away before Rhia noticed. The group continued to the front of the cafeteria and stood nervously near an empty table. One girl sat down, but the rest either looked at their feet or at Rhia. After an awkward wait, Rhia finally declared, "Let's go back to class." The girl stood up. Albert turned Rhia's chair around, and they all dutifully followed Rhia back to their own building on the other side of campus.

I couldn't help thinking how much they didn't belong in the mix of ordinary students. Middle school is where kids are measured and sorted; some will be popular, and some will be pushed to the outer edges of acceptable. Special education students are sorted and pushed out simply because they have something presumably wrong with them.

I watched Rhia during lunch a few days later. She and her friends were sitting at the table close to their classroom eating lunch. Albert made a farting sound with his lips, and everyone except Rhia laughed. When she noticed people laughing, she turned to Tanya and asked, "What are you laughing at?"

Tanya pointed to Albert, then at her butt, then she pinched her nose with her fingers. Rhia laughed.

"You farted!" she said, pointing at Tanya.

Tanya shook her head and pointed at her brother. Rhia said, "He farted!"

She giggled and everyone laughed again.

When Albert made another farting noise, Tanya pointed at him and Rhia instantly understood the joke. "Ewwww!" she said and laughed.

Rhia looked happy eating lunch with her friends, not caring one bit that they were all isolated on the far side of campus where none of her former friends dared to go. Full inclusion for Rhia meant having friends. If Rhia was happy, why did it matter if Rhia was no longer fully included in the larger school community?

I wish I could say I had a breakthrough moment after watching Rhia with her friends, but that would be a lie. I was forced to accept that I had done everything I could to improve Rhia's seventh and eighth grade experience. But accepting the teacher, volunteering in the classroom, researching deaf-blindness, learning from David Brown, providing more snacks for Rhia to keep up her energy, and advocating for her to have an intervener didn't feel like enough. Rhia would spend two years in what I saw was a school program going in the wrong direction. I didn't care that by the eighth grade she was happier, had new friends, liked her teachers, and was learning. None of that mattered compared to the visions I had of her as an adult stuck in a work program where she'd shred paper all day.

Watching Rhia's cousin Lindsay play soccer in the seventh and eighth grade fed my fears. Lindsay went to the Winter Ball with her friends. Lindsay went camping with her great-grandparents (my grandparents), who never invited Rhia to come. It didn't matter that Rhia hated the outdoors and camping would be a type of torture for her—I wanted her invited! I wanted the world to open to her and accept her for who she was and find a way to include her in everything!

There had to be a way to break down the isolation that was building around Rhia. Around me. And around my husband.

Rhia and Rick's relationship changed when she lost her hearing. They went from best buddies running around town in Rick's truck, telling jokes and making up silly songs together, to sitting side by side in silence. Rick would say something to her, and then noticing she hadn't responded, he just stopped talking. Rhia would tell a joke and wait for a response from him, and then tell herself the punch line. Rather than keep trying to understand, Rick became quiet. He didn't stop taking Rhia on errands, but she sat in the back seat and talked to herself while Rick cranked up the music on the radio.

Eventually, that silence touched our marriage. I can't remember exactly when the distance between Rick and me started. When did we stop looking into each other's eyes or reaching across the table to touch the other's hand? When did making love turn from reconnecting to one another into habitual stress relief? When exactly did we start resenting each other more than enjoying each other? I don't remember when it started, but I know it grew at the same pace as Rhia going deaf.

My mother told me you can fall in and out of love several times with the person you're married to so I shouldn't worry. And with the stress around caring for Rhia and no clear explanation of what caused her disabilities, it wasn't surprising Rick and I were feeling distant. Everyone knows that marriage is hard work, and if you don't have the time or energy to work on your marriage, the work can feel impossible.

On one of our rare, just-the-two-of-us weekend trips, I lay awake at night next to my sleeping husband wondering if any parents of a disabled child had time or energy to give to their marriage. Maybe other couples just ride it out, like Rick and I were doing. I looked at his back, which was turned toward me, and reached out to feel his skin. He sighed in his sleep. The only time we shared a bed was on those brief weekends away from our child. At home, Rhia woke up numerous times, and since Rick had a full-time job, I got up to help her. Rather than wake him too, I shut the door on our bedroom and slept down the hall, waiting for Rhia to call me once again during the night.

It can feel impossible to repair a marriage when even the night isn't yours to share with each other.

"Take sign language with me," I said one afternoon at the beginning of Rhia entering the seventh grade.

Rick shook his head. "I'm no good with languages."

"It's movement and expression. Not sound. You're a circus juggler; it should be easy for you to learn."

He shrugged. "Bring me your lessons and I'll practice with you."

Wrapping my arms around him, I looked up into his sad eyes and said, "It could be fun to take the class together."

He hugged me quickly and then turned away before saying, "Who'll watch Rhia while we're both at class?"

He was right that we didn't have childcare for us to go to class together, but it felt like an excuse. Why couldn't we hire a caregiver for two hours one evening a week? If Rick could build a high-speed computer out of spare parts and an outdated manual, why couldn't he learn American Sign Language?

Sadly, I eventually discovered that this resistance to learning sign language is common in parents of children who lose their hearing.

I recently read a 2013 study that showed 90 percent of deaf children born in the United States have hearing parents, and that 70 percent of those parents do not learn sign language. Only 30 percent of hearing parents learn to communicate with their deaf child. I simply can't understand that. How does a parent decide that communicating with their own child is not important?

The study explained some of the reasons parents don't learn sign language, including unconscious bias against deafness (or conscious, which is so much worse), a belief that their child understands enough of what is said to get by, or a reliance on technology and medical interventions, such as the cochlear implant. There is also the very real problem of a parent not having the time to learn. If they have other children who demand their attention or are working long hours to put food on the table, it's hard to keep up with sign language classes.

Learning sign language also means accepting your child's disability, which some parents simply can't do. There is anticipatory grief and a crushing fear that come from knowing your child will struggle their entire life. There is also a sense of guilt, that ongoing belief that maybe you did something to cause your child's disability.

We parents can blame ourselves for everything, from deafness to a hangnail.

I think Rick couldn't accept that Rhia was deaf, so he decided not to learn American Sign Language. When he married me, he truly believed that if he just loved Rhia enough and took care of her, she'd get better. Her ataxia would improve, she'd get stronger, and maybe she'd even see better. Instead, she got worse. She needed to use a wheelchair more often, and then she lost her hearing. There wasn't a damn thing he could do, so instead of accepting that Rhia was deaf he waited for . . . what? A miracle? New technology? A cure for deafness and ataxia?

I am still the only person in our family who has learned sign language. During the holidays as we gather around the table to share food and stories, I use my left hand for my own fork and my right hand to help Rhia eat. When Rick is done, he takes over feeding Rhia so I can chat with relatives and finish my meal. But he can't help Rhia understand the conversations and activities happening at the table.

Someone tells a joke, and everyone laughs. Rhia asks me, "What's so funny?"

I try to explain the joke using my basic sign language skills, adapted for her low vision. She rarely understands the specifics, but when she realizes it was a joke, she'll laugh loudly. By the time I finish interpreting, the conversation has moved to a different topic and I struggle to catch up. I glance at Rhia and see she is lost again, so I interpret again. There is rarely a moment during any holiday that I relax and chat with loved ones. Instead, I'm Rhia's interpreter and full-time helper.

I understand the possible reasons no one else has learned ASL (time, ability, sadness . . .), but I wish someone could take over for me on occasion. I'm tired and, yes, angry, because I'm the only person in the room at every holiday and family event that Rhia can understand.

7

At first I tried studying sign language from Julie, Rhia's teacher of the deaf, learning the same vocabulary Rhia did, but Rhia quickly outpaced me. By the end of the eighth grade, Rhia knew more than five hundred signs. So I signed up for a beginning American Sign Language class at the local community college in the spring of 2010, the year Rhia began high school. The class was taught by an Asian-American deaf man in his mid-thirties. It was a full immersion class, meaning no one was allowed to use spoken language, and our textbook was part workbook exercises and part online videos. I had taken ASL in college twenty years prior to fulfill my foreign language requirement, so I thought with my prior experience and the few signs I had learned from Julie, it would be easy for me to grasp again.

On the first day of class, we watched a video showing a deaf woman using ASL to tell a funny story about chatting with two hearing men at a coffee shop. After the video, our teacher helped us interpret the signs she had used so we could understand the story, signs like "cup," "table," "milk," "sugar," "coffee," "paper," and "pencil." It was actually funny: A deaf woman and a hearing man use pen and paper to communicate.

A second hearing man joins them and all three communicate with pen and paper. When the woman leaves, she looks back and sees that the two men are still using the pen and paper, even though they are both hearing. She laughs and leaves the cafe.

Our teacher asked if anyone wanted to tell the story to the class. Looking around the room at my classmates, I saw that no one raised their hand. The class was mostly young people who I doubted could legally buy alcohol and a few older women like me. I raised my hand to the perceived relief of everyone. With my prior introduction to American Sign Language and my bachelor's degree in drama, I thought it would be easy to tell the story.

Using my whole body to show what happened, I precisely mimicked the movement of opening a sugar packet and pouring it into my too hot coffee, then holding it to my lips to blow on it. I mimed holding a pen, writing words, and then passing it across the table to the other person, who I showed reading the paper and then writing their own response. And when I acted like the woman leaving and then looking behind her at the men still talking to each other with a notepad and pen, I shook my whole body to show laughter. When I finished, the other students started to clap before remembering to wave their hands instead to show a deaf person their appreciation. I grinned, bowed, and looked at my teacher.

He wasn't smiling.

Standing beside me, he explained in very clear sign language and some words written on the whiteboard that all of those large, acting movements I'd done made it look like I was shouting, which was rude. And I had acted out the story rather than using language, again considered extremely rude. As he pointed out everything I'd done wrong, I stared at the floor, embarrassed. I thought I'd done a good job, but I'd clearly disrespected my teacher by acting out a scene instead of trying to use sign language.

I had a lot to learn about American Sign Language and deaf culture.

Despite what you may believe, sign language is not an easy language to learn. Because the language doesn't rely on tone of voice to convey emotion or nuance, you have to use your face, especially your eyebrows. You move your eyebrows upwards to ask a question, something I still forget to do even now. Instead of asking Rhia if she's ready to go, I often tell Rhia she's ready to go simply by not raising my eyebrows. Rhia doesn't respond well to orders, so you'd think I'd remember my eyebrow position by now!

Also, the way you hold your hand can mean different things depending on where you place your hands. The letter A looks like a fist with your thumb on the side of your hand. Aunt is the letter A with your fist moved in a circle at chin height. Apple looks like the letter A but your thumb is out and placed beside your chin. The letter S looks a lot like A, except your thumb is against the front of your fingers. The letter S held against your chest and moved in a circle means you're sorry, but if you open your hand and move it in a circle against your chest that means please. Precision is extremely important.

By the end of that first ASL class, I had learned to sign basic, conversational American Sign Language. Unfortunately,

I could not understand when someone signed basic, conversational American Sign Language to me. It's the same as how someone can learn to speak and read Spanish but has trouble understanding when Spanish is spoken to them. Even today, after many years of using sign language on a daily basis, I have difficulty comprehending a word that is fingerspelled. I can fingerspell while signing to someone else, but when they fingerspell back I'm immediately lost.

My teacher explained this is a common problem with new signers; it takes many years of practice to understand sign language. He encouraged me to continue coming to Deaf Pizza Night and other social events to practice with sign language users and to continue with sign language classes. I took American Sign Language level two, and then I became his teaching assistant the semester after that. Even with all that practice, learning American Sign Language was still challenging. Why couldn't I comprehend what someone was saying to me? I thought of Rick and how he said he was "no good with languages." Maybe I was the same? I'd failed high school Spanish, and I passed my first American Sign Language class with barely a C.

I wouldn't give up, though, because giving up on learning sign language was giving up on communicating with my daughter. She had lost friends because she couldn't talk to them. She couldn't even communicate with members of her own family. But she would always be able to communicate with and be understood by me.

I was still furious she had lost her hearing, but I had accepted it. I would adapt. I would learn. And that was the difference between me and 70 percent of other hearing parents of a deaf child.

Rhia learned American Sign Language with impressive speed, but her hand tremors and poor muscle control prevented her from signing back to a person, even though she fully understood what was being said to her. She combined lip reading with sign language, and if she didn't understand a word, she used pictures and context to figure it out. Comprehending fingerspelling was also hard for her, but that was due to her vision impairment and not lack of knowledge.

Once again, having access to language helped Rhia climb out of her shell just a little. She smiled more and paid closer attention to her lessons at school. Outside of school I became her link to the world, and the more ASL I learned, the more her world grew. It still doesn't matter that I never became fluent in American Sign Language or that on occasion I have to adapt a sign for Rhia's visual needs. I know enough to converse with deaf people at Pizza Night, just as long as they fingerspell slowly. I also bring a pen and paper for backup.

8

Rick and I decided to have Rhia try glasses one more time, hoping it would help her see sign language more easily, especially fingerspelling. I made an appointment with Rhia's ophthalmologist at the University of California, Berkeley, Special Visual Assessment Clinic (SVAC). Still operational today, the clinic specializes in children who are hard to assess in a typical ophthalmologist clinic. The lead doctor, Dr. Bixler, was a master of observation, with an ability to detect the smallest visual reaction in a child who has limited mobility or communication, a skill that would make Sherlock Holmes proud. And there was something about her quiet, low-pitched voice and graceful movements that both soothed and motivated a child with behavioral or developmental challenges. If you wanted an accurate report on the visual needs of a complex, hard-to-assess kid, you went to Dr. Bixler.

Rhia wasn't thrilled by yet another doctor's appointment, even though she liked Dr. Bixler. She cooperated with Dr. Bixler's requests, as she had the last two times she'd been to the clinic, but this time Rhia entertained herself by trying to trick the doctor. At fourteen, Rhia wasn't easily mollified with stickers and cartoons.

I could feel Rhia's thoughts as she touched the cards Dr. Bixler used to test Rhia's visual contrast sensitivity.

. . . the card was on the left, so next time it will be on the right, then it will be on the left again, but the doctor will try to trick me after that and keep it on the left, then go back to the right . . .

It was as if they were playing poker, with Rhia bluffing every move, and Dr. Bixler, a master card player after thirty years, not showing any awareness that she knew Rhia was bluffing.

Dr. Bixler asked Rhia to look at colorful pictures of numbers and then say what the number was. The numbers were at first different from the background color and clearly visible, but after several cards, the shade between the color of the numbers and the background became too similar to easily be detected. The closer the color of the number and the background, the less contrast. After four cards, Rhia squinted and leaned forward to see the number. After six cards, she leaned back in her chair and barely glanced at them, saying random numbers. Her doctor didn't show that she knew Rhia was guessing.

Finally Rhia said in a triumphant voice, "That one doesn't have a number!" She looked at her doctor and smiled. Was she daring Dr. Bixler to contradict her? The number six was visible, but faint in contrast to the similar purple background.

Dr. Bixler just smiled. "Thank you."

Then came the test to determine Rhia's visual field, the area Rhia saw using her peripheral vision. Rhia was asked to look at a single point of light in front of her and then say when she saw another point of light moving closer to her head, without looking away from the light in front of her. The overhead lights in the room were darkened, and Dr. Bixler's assistant moved behind Rhia with a small red light on the end of a long stick. Dr. Bixler sat in front of Rhia and watched Rhia's eyes. The light was slowly moved forward, left side, right side, below, and above. Rhia said, "I see it," and then pointed to the light. The test was repeated with the light brought closer to Rhia so that the peripheral field was narrow. Rhia never saw the light moved above her head and in front until it came down low in front of her nose. This indicated a clear upper field loss. She had no problem seeing the light when it was below her or on either side.

But when the light was at shoulder height on her right side, she again couldn't see it. That didn't stop Rhia from saying, "I see it!" because she knew if the light was on her left side last time it must be on her right side this time.

Dr. Bixler told Rhia she was doing a great job and thanked her. Then she continued with the test.

Despite the game of bluff Rhia played, Dr. Bixler got an accurate reading of Rhia's visual acuity. But when she put glasses on Rhia to try out different lenses, Rhia suddenly couldn't see anything.

"I don't know. I can't see it," she declared, looking down at her lap so the lenses fell out of the frame.

Dr. Bixler smiled and said, "Thank you for telling me."

When the assessment was done, we walked toward the eyeglass counter to pick out new frames. I asked, "Why did her vision get worse with glasses?"

"She's telling me she doesn't want to wear glasses," Dr. Bixler replied calmly.

Rhia refused to pick out new frames, so I chose a purple pair for her, which was her favorite color back then.

Rhia's functional vision had improved from 20/600 two years ago to 20/400 (it was 20/1000 when she was first diagnosed with optic atrophy). She still had optic atrophy, so the cause of her vision impairment hadn't changed, but apparently her brain's ability to process visual information had. Was it age and maturity? Her brain's natural ability to adapt? Who knew? I was just so happy to get some good news for a change!

Now I had to figure out how to get Rhia to wear the damn glasses.

The doctor suggested we ease into them rather than have her wear them all the time. Rhia liked to read; perhaps looking at her books would be the perfect time to try her new glasses. She was also encouraged to wear them at school when doing schoolwork.

Her teacher had more success than me in getting Rhia to wear glasses. That's to be expected; no fourteen-year-old wants to do what their mother says. Eventually Rhia kept her glasses on while sitting at her desk at school, but the moment she finished her schoolwork, she removed them.

She did not wear them when people spoke to her using sign language.

9

Rick, Laurent, and I had to make another important medical decision when Rhia was in middle school, this one with a greater impact on Rhia's life.

Should Rhia get a cochlear implant?

Rhia's audiologist suggested the implant as a way for Rhia to regain some, if not most, of her hearing. This should have been an easy decision. With an implant, Rhia and Rick could tell silly jokes to each other again and rebuild their relationship. She could understand people when they talked to her and maybe reconnect with old friends from Oak Manor.

Would a cochlear implant help Rhia communicate more easily and therefore experience less isolation? Yes! Then let's do the implant.

But just like most decisions about disabilities, there is never a simple yes or no.

A cochlear implant is an electronic device that stimulates the inner ear so the person hears sounds. It is made of three parts, and from the outside looks like the type of behind-the-ear hearing aid that most people have seen. The external part is the processor, which has a microphone and a computer to pick up sound and translate it into electrical signals. These signals travel up a wire to the transmitting coil, which is attached to the side of the head by a magnet. The signals travel through electrodes implanted into the inner ear, which then are interpreted by the brain as verbal speech or other sounds in the environment. It doesn't provide perfect hearing, but a cochlear implant typically restores enough hearing for a person to comprehend speech.

Cochlear implants are especially beneficial for people who once had hearing and then for whatever reason became deaf. The success rate for people who learned spoken language is particularly high, and cochlear implants are also recommended for people like Rhia with sensorineural hearing loss. The process requires surgery to implant electrodes in the brain, and like all surgeries there can be complications. Cochlear implants don't work for everyone, so there was a chance Rhia would go through surgery, followed by months of therapy to train her brain to understand the meaning of the sounds she was hearing, and still be unable to hear speech. Sounds may continue to be a rumble of disconnected tones, only now amplified into a cacophony. And she would still need to wear a hearing aid behind one of her ears, which she barely tolerated. The outcome was unknown, particularly as we still didn't know what caused her hearing loss, the hypotonia, her low vision, and the ataxia. If we knew what was causing her illness we could all make a well-informed decision. Not having a diagnosis made every choice feel like we were just flipping a coin.

We were also inadvertently thrown into the debate about the ethics of cochlear implants and deaf culture. Sign language is a unique, living language that has culture and community built into it. Hearing people often judge the deaf and wonder why most deaf people want to keep using sign language, which keeps them isolated from the larger, hearing world. We wonder, "Why don't you want to have more opportunity and access to the privileges we hearing people enjoy? Why are you choosing to be disabled?"

But most deaf people don't feel disabled because they are part of a strong community. This community has its own language and leaders and history. We can't just ask what a deaf person will gain from becoming hearing; we also need to ask: What does a deaf person lose if they can hear?

Laurent, Rick, and I struggled with the choice. At first Rick wanted to do it, while Laurent and I weren't so sure. After more research, we agreed that a cochlear implant was a good idea for Rhia, regardless of the outcome. She used to have hearing. She knew spoken language. She understood sign language, but her hand tremors made signing challenging so she was still isolated from other deaf people. It was worth the risk.

But ultimately, the decision was made by Rhia because she simply refused to wear hearing aids. If she couldn't keep simple hearing aids in her ears, then she was ineligible for the implant. It was obvious she would never tolerate a large hearing aid behind her ear connected to wires that were connected to her brain. Why put her through the surgery, then?

It was worth a try though, so Rhia's teachers, both dads, and I begged, coaxed, encouraged, threatened, ordered, and bribed Rhia to keep her hearing aids in. We were all invested in Rhia regaining her hearing so she wouldn't be isolated. We tried easing her into wearing the hearing aids by starting with a few minutes and working up to an hour and eventually the whole day. We tried stickers and special treats. Rick made "TV dollars" so Rhia earned time to watch her favorite movies.

Rhia simply yanked the hearing aids out of her ears and tossed them on the floor. Or she threw them out the car window, left them on the playground, and once dropped them into the toilet after having a bowel movement. The battle continued for two long years with tears on every side, but eventually we all agreed the battle had been lost. Rhia would not wear hearing aids and therefore would not get a cochlear implant.

Sometimes I regret that choice. I should have pushed harder. I should have found a way to keep those damn hearing aids plugged into Rhia's ears. Not getting a cochlear implant made Rhia completely cut off from both worlds, hearing and deaf. If I had stood firm and forced her to get an implant, there was an excellent chance she would now be able to communicate with people directly.

But then I laugh. No one forces Rhia to do anything. I may be stubborn, but she is unstoppable.

10

My mom and I were drinking tea at my kitchen table when we heard Rhia yell.

"Argh!"

My mom looked up at me, her eyebrows raised in concern. I kept sipping my tea.

"This is impossible!" Rhia yelled.

We heard what sounded like a heavy book being hurled against the wall, then another "Argh!" from Rhia.

My mom set her cup down and looked in the direction of Rhia's room.

I kept sipping my tea.

"How can I do this if my stupid ataxia won't go away?" Rhia shouted.

My mom looked back at me. "Is she okay?"

I nodded. "Yeah. She's fine."

There was another loud bang, and then more shouting from Rhia. If she knew any swear words she'd be swearing like a sailor who'd been denied shore leave.

"What is she doing?" my mom asked.

"Making her bed."

Rhia yelled, "The stupid blankets won't stay up!"

My mom raised her eyebrows. "Making her bed?"

"Yep." I kept sipping my tea.

"Sounds awfully loud. Does she need help?"

"Nope."

My mom looked back toward the bedroom, where the sounds of Rhia struggling with her bed grew louder. "Are you sure?"

"Yep."

Rhia yelled, "Where did my pillow go?"

My mom glanced back at me, then picked up her cup and quietly drank her tea. But her entire body stayed tense as she listened to the shouts and banging coming from Rhia's room.

After several more minutes of complaints, shouts, and struggles, Rhia yelled, "Mom, I made my bed."

I took another sip of tea, set my cup down, and walked to her bedroom. My mom quickly followed.

Rhia stood beside her newly made bed. Her blankets were bunched up and crooked, but the pillows were in place. "See. I made my bed."

"Good job, honey," I said.

"Can you help me pull up the blanket? It's touching the floor."

"Sure." I reached under the comforter and pulled the blanket up flat on the bed, then smoothed it neatly.

"Great job," I said, giving Rhia a hug.

Rhia's face was flushed and she wiped her brow. "Whew. I need a drink."

As the three of us headed to the kitchen, my mom asked, "Is making the bed always so loud?"

"Yep," I said.

Grief

1

Way back when Rhia was in preschool and we moved into our little house in Lakeport, I decided we needed a cat. A house isn't a home without a cat staring at you from the front window when you arrive. So we went to the local animal shelter to hunt for the right cat for our two-person family. A cat that was fluffy and friendly, preferably orange to make it easier for Rhia to see. A cat that wouldn't be afraid of a toddler who fell down a lot. And not a kitten; kittens required as much if not more potty training than Rhia did.

The cat shelter was a large concrete room with fluorescent lights and a steel door. Three rows of wire cages were stacked one on top of the other almost to the ceiling, and in each cage was a cat. Some of the cages held two cats or several small kittens. There was just enough room to wheel Rhia's stroller between the rows.

"All of these are up for adoption," said the shelter attendant, a young woman in muddy overalls and rubber boots. "Look around and let me know if you see one you like."

There were so many cats meowing and hissing and purring and growling, I had no idea how to choose the right one. Some cats hid in the corner of their cage while others pressed themselves against the wire urgently, as if hoping if they squeezed hard enough they'd be free. Many of the cats slept soundly, not caring about the woman walking up and down the aisles, holding the cheerful toddler. Kittens played the best they could in tiny spaces; even in a cage, babies want to play.

There was one large, fluffy, bright orange cat who caught Rhia's attention. Instead of frantically pressing against the cage, he purred and rubbed against it, first one side of his long body and then the other. Rhia pointed and said, "Dat cat!"

The attendant took him out of his cage and carried him to the meet-and-greet room, a small room with a couch and a rug. The orange cat jumped onto the couch and purred louder, as if inviting us to join him.

"He's a popular one," the attendant said. "He already has two people lined up to adopt him."

I stroked his head. "I can see why. He's a lover."

I told the attendant to write us down as a third option if the other people didn't work out. Rhia didn't understand why we weren't bringing "Orange Cat" home with us immediately and began to cry. I explained he'd already been chosen by another family, but as any three-year-old would, she complained about not bringing Orange Cat home "now!"

The next day I went back to the shelter on my own, leaving Rhia with my mom. The cat shelter was just as depressing as before, and there were so many cats no one wanted. It wasn't a no-kill shelter either; most of these animals would be euthanized within the month. For some cats, I could be their last chance to find a home. Swallowing a lump of sadness, I hunted for my perfect cat.

Still feeling sad and angry about how we humans treat animals, I stopped in front of the cage of a gray, tortoiseshell cat who was sitting quietly, watching me. She wasn't purring or meowing or pressing against the walls of her cage. She just sat there watching me pass by. When I walked near her cage again, she reached out one paw through the gaps in the cage, as if saying, "I'm your cat." I stopped and carefully touched the back of her paw. She didn't flinch, pull away, or try to scratch me. She just kept looking at me.

I told the attendant I wanted her. The attendant said, "That's great. This one is due to be euthanized in two days."

She'd already been spayed, so all I had to do was pay the adoption fee and she was all mine. I returned later that afternoon with a cat carrier I borrowed from my mom, and by dinner time, she was home. Rhia forgot all about Orange Cat and fell in love with "The Cat."

I named her Dharma because she reminded me to look for the small joys when life gets overwhelming. Dharma curling up against my belly at night helped me sleep, and watching her patiently play with the ribbon Rhia kept dangling in front of Dharma's nose made me smile. I knew Dharma was a grown cat who didn't really want to play, but she seemed to enjoy how much Rhia was delighted. She even put up with how terrible Rhia was at petting her. In the eight years Dharma lived with us, Rhia never figured out how to pet Dharma's fur down rather than up. Dharma never complained and never scratched Rhia.

When Rick moved in with us two years later, Dharma gained another lap. She liked to climb on top of Rick's shoulder whenever he sat down and then lick his bald head. She brought us gifts of dead mice and half-murdered birds and appeared offended when we didn't consume them immediately.

Eight years later, I broke Dharma's heart.

Rhia had always had hay fever, but when she turned eleven her symptoms became much worse. Her eyes and nose dripped constantly, and she developed a cough. Nothing helped her feel better. Finally we took her to an allergist, who diagnosed her with allergies to dust, oak trees, and cats.

"This is one of the worst cases of cat allergies I've seen in a long time," he explained. "I advise you to get rid of your cat."

"What if we keep the cat off of her and vacuum everything?" I asked.

"You can try, but you'll be vacuuming every day."

"What about an air filter to trap the hair?"

"It's not the hair that's the problem. It's the saliva. Cats lick everything. I really think you should just get rid of the cat or keep it outdoors at all times."

Dharma was probably ten years old (the shelter thought she was two when we adopted her) and had enjoyed an indoor-outdoor lifestyle. I doubted forcing her to live outside full time was going to work.

Of all the diagnoses we've had to cope with, Rhia's cat allergy was the hardest. It is the one medical condition I resent the most even today. I could cope with her blindness and deafness and the ataxia and hypotonia and the developmental delays, but the cat allergy was infuriating. I chose to get a cat because I love cats, and now that cat . . . that little piece of happiness I chose for myself, was being taken away. I could keep Dharma, but that would put Rhia's health at risk; she had enough to deal with! But goddamn it! This wasn't fair! Why cats? Why not dogs or horses or rabbits? Why did I have to give up another thing that brought me happiness just to keep my daughter safe?

Bringing Dharma back to the shelter wasn't an option; she'd be euthanized quickly. Thankfully Tama, my dear friend who took us to Disneyland, once again came to the rescue, saying she would adopt my cat.

Dharma rode in the back of my van inside a large animal carrier. A regular cat carrier was too small to get her in because she fought furiously every time I tried to bundle her into the smaller official cat cage. I think Dharma had PTSD from the cage at the animal shelter. I borrowed the type of cage used to transport small livestock, like a lamb, so Dharma couldn't loop her limbs around the edges of the doorway. She yowled for the entire three-hour drive to Tama's house, and I cried for most of it. No matter how much I tried to explain, Dharma kept yowling. Of course she did; she's a cat, and there was no way she'd understand I put her in a cage and then the car because Rhia was allergic to her.

Tama and I carried the animal cage into her living room, set it down, and opened the door. Dharma burst out and squeezed herself under a bookcase, refusing to come out. I stayed for an hour, thanking Tama and hoping I could pet Dharma once more to say goodbye. Eventually I had to drive home, this time in a quiet car with an empty cage. I cried even harder. Tama told me that Dharma came out from under the bookcase to eat, but for two days mostly stayed hidden. Eventually she allowed Tama to stroke her, and in a week she was sitting on Tama's lap.

When I saw Dharma a few months later, Dharma just glared at me, turned her back, and left the room. I would never be forgiven.

In Buddhist theology, Dharma is the way, the path of life. Life is joy and intense pain. It's no one's fault. It isn't a punishment; it's just the way life is. The more we cling to people, animals, and objects, the harder life becomes.

Never name your cat Dharma.

2

It would be a thousand times easier to make decisions about Rhia's medical care if we only had more information about the cause of Rhia's disabilities. I was sick and tired of managing her symptoms based on nothing more than intuition and vague recommendations from specialists who were also going by intuition. It looked like Rhia had ataxia telangiectasia, but she didn't. It also wasn't Friedreich's ataxia. There was no brain tumor or lesion or anything to explain her motor function decline and hearing loss. I spent hours online hunting for "maybes" and only scaring myself with the outcomes of each "maybe" disease it might be.

At first we wondered if it was the jaundice. Laurent went to the University of California, San Francisco, where Rhia had been born, to find answers. After several weeks of requests for copies of Rhia's medical records, followed by direct threats of legal action, he got all of the documentation from her birth. We looked at the chart notes and test results from 1995 when she was two weeks old. The bilirubin in her blood had been so high it almost killed her. Did the hospital make a mistake by letting it get so high? Could her disabilities have been prevented?

Rhia was ten when Laurent discovered a condition called kernicterus, which is caused by brain damage from high bilirubin, which is what causes jaundice. While looking up kernicterus information during one of my late night internet hunts, I discovered a medical conference about kernicterus happening that summer at the Hyatt Hotel in Richmond, Virginia. With a grant from the Regional Center, I flew across the country to find out more. In my carry-on bag was an eight-pound file of Rhia's medical records, including all the notes from the hospital on the day she was born.

It was my first medical conference and the first time I'd sat in a room filled with other parents seeking answers for their child's illness. The parents with young children sat on the edge of the seats and took detailed notes of everything the lecturer said. The parents with children teenaged or older sat back in their chairs with folded arms and nodded now and then to show they were listening. I started by sitting up front taking a lot of notes, but by the third lecture from another esteemed medical expert, I too leaned back in my chair without bothering to take the pen from my purse. It was clear from the information I'd gathered on the first day of the conference that Rhia did not have kernicterus.

But I had to be sure, so I reserved a time to discuss her case with one of the world's leaders on kernicterus. The doctor was a woman in her mid-forties with shoulder-length bobbed hair wearing a red, short-sleeved blouse. As she looked at some of the documents I'd brought, I told her about Rhia. After a few minutes, the doctor took off her reading glasses and confirmed that Rhia didn't have kernicterus. "Your daughter has something progressive. Kernicterus damage is a single event that causes brain damage. It doesn't get worse over time, at least not like your daughter." She smiled kindly as she passed the papers back to me. "I wish I had more information for you, but at least you can cross off kernicterus. Good luck in your search."

I went back to my hotel room and cried.

Later that night was the opening reception of the conference, which I forced myself to attend despite my feelings of dissolution. I was late. The servers were bringing dinners to the table as the opening speaker began showing his presentation slides. In the back of the room was a table with two open chairs, so I walked to it and asked if I could join them. I didn't know the table was reserved for the medical doctors in attendance and they didn't tell me not to sit. It was an extremely fortunate mistake.

Sitting at the table was Terence Sanderson, a world-renowned movement disorders specialist who practiced at Stanford University Medical Center. After introductions, during which I discovered my mistake and offered to find another table (they all said I should stay), another doctor asked me about Rhia.

"I came hoping to find some answers but it looks like another dead end." Pulling out a picture of Rhia, I handed it to the doctor. "This is Rhia. She's why I'm here."

He smiled. "She's beautiful." He passed it to another doctor, who then passed it to Dr. Sanderson.

Dr. Sanderson smiled, handed the photo back to me, and then asked, "What are her symptoms?"

A waiter set my chicken and rice dinner in front of me, and as we ate, I told them about Rhia's ataxia, hypotonia, optic nerve hypoplasia, and developmental delay (she could still hear at this time). They all had questions. What was her height and weight? Stamina? Strength? Type of nystagmus? Genetic background? Skin coloring? Does she easily bruise? As they asked questions, I realized that Rhia's case had become the main focus of the table, as if they'd been presented with a puzzle that needed immediate solving but some of the pieces were missing.

Scientists, whether medical or other, love a good puzzle—the more mysterious, the better. And Rhia was the ultimate puzzle.

Dr. Sanderson gave me his card and said to call for an appointment. There was a waiting list of several months, but he said he'd tell his assistant to put us at the top of the list. He was intrigued by Rhia, and he wanted to meet her.

Sometimes I imagine doctors talking about Rhia at dinner parties like she's some kind of exotic mystery. The young girl with multiple disabling symptoms that on their own mean something but when put together in one person make absolutely no sense. There is nothing any specialist or expert can point to and say, "There! That is the reason." She is blind due to damaged optic nerves, but what is causing the ataxia? Optic nerve hypoplasia doesn't present with ataxia. Her cerebellum shows deterioration, but what is causing the deterioration? Her blood work is perfect. There are zero markers for anything we can identify. And what has happened to her hearing? Her ears and nerves look fine, so why did she become deaf?

Dr. Sanderson thought she had something called ataxia telangiectasia, which was lethal. But all the blood work came back negative. Not ataxia telangiectasia. Relief. Also frustration.

"It looks like AT but isn't AT." He scowled at his computer screen, where the lab results glowed.

I looked at Rhia, who was now scowling at the doctor. She was hungry and wanted to go home.

"What does Rhia have?"

"I don't know . . ."

He ordered more tests and another MRI, which required Rhia and me to travel three hours back and forth from Ukiah. I was willing, but Rhia was quickly losing patience. Dr. Sanderson was determined to understand the cause of Rhia's condition.

And then after three years, during one more appointment, he swiveled his rolling stool to face me and asked, "Have you ever heard of mitochondrial disease?"

I shook my head, then said, "I know what mitochondria is from biology class, but not mitochondrial disease."

"It's a new field of medicine. We're just now learning about the effects of mitochondria on disease and what to look for. Like I said, it's new, but the doctor I want Rhia to see is the expert."

3

How many cells are in your body? Billions? Each one of those cells combines with other cells that have the same job: make a part of your body. Cells create your skin, your bones, your eyeballs, and your brain. Different cells bond together to flow through arteries, carrying oxygen to each and every one of the parts that are you. Nothing in your body is created without cells. Inside each of those cells is a nucleus that carries the information telling the cell what to become. The cells that make your tongue are unable to make your lips.

Cells need fuel to create your body and keep it functioning. So we eat and drink and exercise to give our cells the energy they need to thrive. But how do the cells get the energy from the food you eat? They can't just absorb the banana pudding you ate for dessert through their membranes and get fuel. Some of you probably remember learning about the Krebs cycle, or citric acid cycle, in high school biology. A very simple explanation is that the food we eat is transformed through various chemical reactions to create acetyl-CoA, which is transformed into ATP, which provides energy to the cells. The actual process is far more complicated, but if you want to understand every step (there are ten) and all of the chemical reactions that fuel your cells, go find your biology textbook. The vital element of the Krebs cycle to help understand Rhia's disabilities are the mitochondria, found in almost every cell in your body. The mitochondria are what create ATP. Without the mitochondria, your cells would slowly starve and you would eventually die.

The discovery of how the mitochondria can malfunction and cause cell damage leading to disease was a brand-new field of research in 2008. Researchers knew about the mitochondria, of course, but until then didn't have the tools or ability to discover exactly how the mitochondria functioned and why they sometimes stopped working. But the most astonishing discovery was that the mitochondria have their own DNA (labeled mDNA). The DNA that codes our cells to become specific types of body structures interacts with the mDNA of the mitochondria, but does not directly order the mitochondria to do their job in a certain way. Instead, the DNA tells the cell what to do, and then the mDNA decides how to create the type of fuel that cell will need. An amazing theory is that because mitochondria have their own DNA, millions of years ago they were once individual organisms that joined with a different type of organism to form a symbiotic organism that became the creature that left the primordial oceans to become . . . us.

Another interesting discovery at that time was that mitochondria are passed down from only the mother. We get our DNA from both parents, which creates our unique body types and personalities. But our mDNA is only passed to us from our mothers; the father's mDNA is ignored. Mitochondria are matrilineal. In fact, geneticists can now trace your matrilineal lineage back thousands of generations and tell you in which part of the world your original ancestors evolved based on the type of mDNA you carry.

It may have been beneficial for our primordial ancestors to evolve into one organism in the great ocean of Earth's past, but it also began a complex system with millions of opportunities to break down. Every exchange between DNA and mDNA can create a mistake. That mistake can multiply, leading to disease. There's a theory that mDNA is potentially more sensitive to environmental harm than DNA (as of this writing, this theory is being studied). Toxins and other stressors harm cells, which in turn disrupt the mitochondria. When a cell changes, for good or bad, the information in the mitochondria changes too. And the mitochondria can become impaired and negatively impact the cell. Ordinary aging also impairs mitochondria, and there is ongoing research exploring ways of supporting mitochondrial health to reduce aging.

Parkinson's, diabetes, Alzheimer's, and Huntington's are diseases with suspected mitochondrial triggers. And the list of known mitochondrial diseases is long.

- Leber's hereditary optic neuropathy
- Leigh syndrome
- Mitochondrial neurogastrointestinal encephalopathy
- MERRF syndrome
- MELAS syndrome
- And on and on and on . . .

I learned all of this in a flurry of online research as I waited for the appointment with the mitochondrial specialist at Stanford. Rhia had all of the markers for a mitochondrial disease: cerebellar atrophy and hypoplasia, ataxia, vision impairment, hearing impairment, hypotonia, and developmental delay. Rhia must have a mitochondrial disease! It's the only thing that could explain the degeneration. Her labs also showed markers, including high lactate. And with all other possibilities exhausted, it was the logical answer. But which type? And what did it mean for Rhia?

Dr. Graham was a quiet man in his mid-forties with round glasses and a warm smile. He sat on a low stool and rolled himself next to Rhia before introducing himself directly to her. Rhia studied him carefully and closely, deciding if she would like him or not, which is what she does with all new doctors. As Dr. Graham tested her reflexes with what looked like a tuning fork and then asked Rhia to reach out and touch his finger with her own, he slowly drew Rhia out of her cautious shell. After about twenty minutes he had her chatting and smiling. If Rhia trusted him, I decided I would too.

He finished the exam by watching Rhia walk down the hallway while holding my hand for stability. When Rhia was safely buckled into her wheelchair in the exam room, he turned his attention to me and tried to answer every question I had gathered from my internet research.

I began with the most important question first. "Do you think she has a mitochondrial disease?"

"Probably. It looks like mitochondrial disease, but I need to run some tests to make sure," he responded.

"What kind of tests? A muscle biopsy?"

"Let's start with blood work before a biopsy. I want to avoid creating extra stress for Rhia."

No wonder Rhia liked him.

Dr. Graham explained the particular mitochondrial blood tests he wanted and what each test looked for. He hoped to get everything accomplished with one blood draw rather than coming back for multiple blood draws, so he ordered a long list that included the starting tests for mitochondrial disease, as well as a few that weren't commonly ordered but could provide important information.

When I explained to Rhia she needed to go downstairs for a blood draw, she crossed her arms tightly against her chest and said, "No. I'm not gonna!"

Dr. Graham said, "I'm sorry, Rhia. I know it's hard. But I really need you to do this so I can figure out how to help you."

I interpreted what he said. Rhia glared at him then at me, then she looked at the wall. She relaxed her arms and sighed. "Fine. But I don't like it!"

Dr. Graham thanked her directly by signing, "Thank you."

"We should have the results in a few weeks," he said to me. "I hope to have some answers for you soon."

Answers. I loved the sound of that word.

He called four weeks later. Every test he ordered, other than high lactate, came back negative. He sounded as baffled as Dr. Sanderson had been.

Dr. Graham explained that according to the Bernier criteria, a scaling system based on evidence provided by clinical and visible symptoms, Rhia had mitochondrial disease. In fact, the

Bernier criteria upgraded her from "probable" to "definite." But there was still no actual, physical proof he could point to in her cells or blood, which meant there was no specific diagnosis of the type of mitochondrial disease she had.

"Unfortunately, that means we do need to get a muscle biopsy," he said.

"Surgery?" I asked.

"Yes. The surgeon will take a small sample of muscle from her quadricep as well as a skin sample. If her muscle cells show red-ragged fibers, that will prove without a doubt mitochondrial disease and can help tell us what type."

I'd read about red-ragged fibers, which are clumps of dead mitochondria that accumulate along the edges of cells. But surgery . . . I dreaded holding her down again while she screamed. "Is that absolutely necessary?"

"If I can figure out the type of mitochondrial disease Rhia has, then I can find a treatment. There isn't a cure, but there are newer treatments all the time that help the symptoms. Believe me, I don't recommend invasive testing for any of my patients unless absolutely necessary."

Silently apologizing to Rhia, I said, "Okay. Let's schedule surgery."

Six weeks later, we drove to Stanford again, this time with Aunt Margie and cousin Lindsay. The four of us had a wonderful time exploring the Stanford mall, where Lindsay introduced Rhia to the joy that is Abercrombie & Fitch. *So this is what a typical sixteen-year-old does*, I thought, watching Lindsay try on different outfits in the overly perfumed store.

That night we stayed in a nice hotel near the hospital where we ate dinner by the pool. Rhia was ecstatic to have her best friend so close. Occasionally she'd reach out to hold Lindsay's hand. Margie hugged Rhia and helped with a drink or finding a book. She was also an incredible support for me, reminding me of details the doctors had said and finding my purse when I couldn't see it six inches from my ankle. Thursday evening I took a break and had a glass of wine by the turquoise pool, comforted by the fact that Margie and Lindsay were there watching over Rhia.

Friday was the actual procedure. We all woke up at five, scooped up Rhia, and then drove one mile to the hospital, where we rolled her in her wheelchair to the Surgery Center. Rhia was tearful and frightened, but every time Lindsay held her hand or smiled at her, Rhia smiled back. Unfortunately, they wouldn't let Lindsay into the pre-op area because she wasn't eighteen. But Margie came, helping me stay strong, so I could help Rhia stay calm.

I wondered if they were told what happened the last time Rhia got frightened and how much getting punched hurt. The last time we were at the Surgery Center, Rhia fought and cried so hard that one of the nurses had to leave the room in tears. I know we upset their schedule, but they didn't rush us. We took it very slow this time; the nurse had me take the lead on showing Rhia what was happening. The resident doctor interviewed me from the doorway so Rhia wouldn't feel crowded, and then he had me put the numbing cream on Rhia's arm so she wouldn't be frightened by a stranger doing it. Rhia drank the medicine the anesthesiologist gave her, and in about ten minutes she was stoned enough to lie back and relax. I walked with her as the resident doctor and two nurses wheeled her bed down the hall, but when I let go of her hand at the door to the surgery, there was no fighting.

I waited in the cafeteria with Margie and Lindsay, drinking decent coffee and fighting the desire to run down the hallway to rescue my child. I hated the waiting. My child was somewhere in a room full of strangers, completely helpless, and I was just trusting these people not to hurt her. I did trust them. Lucille Packard Children's Hospital was one of the best in the nation, and Dr. Graham said he had complete trust in the surgeon. And we'd get answers! Answers became my mantra that day.

Finally the procedure was over, and the surgeon came out to see us. Rhia had done great and was in recovery. Margie and I went to post-op to be there when Rhia woke up. When I took Rhia's hand and leaned close to say hello, she opened her eyes and then kissed me. After that, she went back to sleep. I tickled, stroked, kissed, and massaged her, but she refused to wake up.

The nurse just shrugged. "It happens sometimes. Her body really likes the medication."

She was clearly exhausted, and after a fifteen-hour fast in preparation for the surgery, out of fuel. At last, after two hours, Rhia woke up enough to sit up and drink some juice. Once that happened, the nurses let her go. She slept almost the entire three-hour ride home.

Rick was waiting for us when we got home. Margie and Lindsay helped us unload the car and get Rhia settled on the couch, where Lindsay coaxed Rhia into eating a little yogurt.

Before they left that night, I said to Lindsay, "I don't care if you have school or a job or whatever. You're coming again the next time Rhia has to go to the hospital or have any kind of surgery."

Lindsay smiled and shrugged. "No problem."

I hugged her, again saying thank you. Then I hugged Margie. "I couldn't have done this without you."

"That's what family is for," she said.

The muscle biopsy came back negative. Dr. Graham was even more baffled. No specific diagnosis, and no answers.

4

A CHILD WITH A LIFE-THREATENING ILLNESS GETS TO have a wish come true. Rhia decided she wanted to meet her favorite singer, Laurie Berkner. And so, the Make-A-Wish organization got to work making Rhia's biggest dream come true. They don't have magic wands, but they do have excellent contacts and enough financial donations to make just about anything happen.

Laurie Berkner was playing a concert at the Lincoln Center for the Performing Arts in New York City, so I got one of my dreams too: a trip to the Big Apple. We also got to ride all the way from Ukiah to San Francisco International Airport in a white stretch limousine, another fantasy of mine. Rhia hated the limo; it was too big inside. She refused to play "Where should we sit now?" with me and only yelled, "No!" as I tried different spots in the large passenger area. She finally relaxed when we found the snacks.

We flew nonstop from San Francisco to New York City, then rode in a smaller, black limousine to our hotel in Manhattan, just two blocks from Central Park. We were greeted by several gifts from Laurie Berkner spread out on the bed: two books, music CDs, a concert DVD, and a stuffed pink pig in a Laurie Berkner T-shirt.

Rhia giggled, put the pig on her head, and started singing the song, *Laurie's got a Pig on her Head.*

Who is Laurie Berkner and why was fifteen-year-old Rhia obsessed with her?

Laurie Berkner is a singer/songwriter for children, but unlike some in that genre, her songs are well-crafted and don't drive parents insane listening to them over and over. Rhia discovered Laurie Berkner in kindergarten on Noggin, a children's television station popular in the early 2000s. Laurie and her band performed funny, danceable songs between episodes of *Little Bear*, *Franklin*, and other cartoons. Rhia loved Laurie's music as much as her favorite cartoons, and soon we had a collection of every one of Laurie Berkner's CDs. We sang along to her music in the car during the long trips to Stanford, learning every song by heart. Rhia never outgrew Laurie Berkner and remembered all of Laurie's songs even after she lost her hearing. Laurie Berkner was Rhia's Beatles, Madonna, and Britney Spears combined, and in 2010, she met her music idol.

Rhia was given three days in Manhattan and plenty of spending money to enjoy it. But first she had to get used to the noise and chaos of a metropolis. I was hungry to explore the city I had dreamed of since childhood, but I knew we had to go slow. Rhia could hear and feel the rumbling vibrations of loud trucks and traffic, and the packed sidewalks were just a blur of movement to her. I pushed her wheelchair carefully as we walked toward Central Park on our first day in New York. The flow of thousands of people walking on the sidewalk swept us along, and I immediately learned to keep my pace with the crowd or be shoved against the side of a building to clear the way.

Rhia yelled that she wanted to go back to the room, but I thought, *Don't stop and don't fight the current, no matter how much Rhia yells she wants to go back.*

Four long city blocks later, we arrived at Central Park. As we walked along one curving path lined with tall trees just beginning to bud, the roar of idling cars on jammed streets faded and I heard birds singing. Hundreds of people were there too, but the pace of the flow slowed. I sighed, content to travel through Central Park as long as Rhia would allow.

She lasted about ten minutes.

"I want to go back!" she yelled, gripping the armrests of her chair.

I stopped, turned around, and gently squeezed her shoulder to show her I understood. Stepping back into the flow of people, I quickened my pace as we walked to our hotel, and when we reached the front door, I smoothly exited the "stream," as if I'd lived in New York for years.

New York was exhilarating, but Rhia looked terrified. She gripped her armrests from the lobby all the way to the fifteenth-floor room. I understood why; she was in a wheelchair being pushed through crowds that loomed above her head down streets that echoed with constant noise that she couldn't identify. Her fear made sense, but I was determined. There was no way we were going to spend our entire New York trip stuck in the hotel room.

After a break, I convinced her to go for a walk again, this time around the block. She gripped her armrests the entire time but didn't yell to go back. We made the block, took a break in the hotel lobby, then went out for another walk, this time up the street away from Central Park. After three blocks she wanted to go back, so I found a spot to exit the flow of people, waited for an opportunity, then entered the flow going back to the hotel.

At one street crossing, her chair lurched forward as her front wheels became stuck in a grate next to the sidewalk. The light changed and cars began to move, but we were still in the road. I yanked on her chair again, trying to pry the wheels loose, but it wouldn't budge. Suddenly a man grabbed the front of her chair, lifted it up, and smoothly pulled it onto the sidewalk. Before I could say thank you, he was gone, lost in the crowd that never stops moving.

That night as Rhia slept in her double bed, surrounded by gifts from Laurie Berkner, I stared out the window. We were fifteen stories up, but buildings still rose high above us. Mesmerized by the lights of the cars in constant motion, I said out loud, "I'm really in New York City!"

This Make-A-Wish trip was for Rhia, and I was there to be her support. I knew we wouldn't see the Statue of Liberty or the Empire State Building or even the Metropolitan Museum of Art, but just being in Manhattan felt incredible. Ever since I was eight years old practicing my Oscar acceptance speech in the bathroom mirror, I'd dreamed of going to New York City. I never acted on Broadway, but I finally did make it to the city of my dreams.

Turning to look at my sleeping daughter, I whispered, "Thank you."

The next day was Laurie Berkner's concert. A black limousine picked us up at our hotel and drove us to the Lincoln Center, where we were met by a volunteer from Make-A-Wish. We were given our tickets and backstage passes and then escorted to our seats, which were in the back of the theater in what I'm sure was a very expensive box. However, it wasn't going to work for Rhia.

"Rhia is visually impaired, so being this far from the stage won't work. She won't see anything here," I said.

The young woman was flustered. "Oh . . . Um . . . I didn't know that. Um . . ." She glanced at Rhia's wheelchair. "There aren't any wheelchair seats closer to the stage."

"She can transfer from her chair to a seat. Are there any seats closer to the stage?"

It was fifteen minutes until curtain time, but I was determined that Rhia would see Laurie on that stage! The woman pulled out her walkie-talkie and got to work. With five minutes until show time, I wheeled Rhia's chair to the second row from the stage and then half carried her from her chair to her seat. Our liaison rolled Rhia's chair out of the aisle as I took my seat next to Rhia two seconds before Laurie walked on the stage.

"There she is," I said to Rhia, pointing at Laurie. But Rhia didn't need me to point her out. Laurie stood about twenty feet from us wearing a bright green T-shirt and orange pants and holding a guitar. Her curly hair shone under the spotlights. Rhia clapped her hands and grinned.

All around us, hundreds of children clapped and shouted, "Laurie!" I heard several children scream. It was just like the videos of women screaming at a Beatles concert and just as high-pitched. Plugging my ears with my fingers, I laughed. I have never seen so many three- to eight-year-old children so happy. And Rhia was just as ecstatic. I think if Santa Claus had walked in the room with a bag of toys, every child in that place would have pushed him down to get to Laurie.

When the hour-long concert finished, our liaison brought Rhia's wheelchair. We then were escorted backstage to meet Laurie Berkner and her band.

Laurie sat on a couch with a young girl, another Make-A-Wish child, who I think was about seven. Laurie waved at Rhia and I rolled her wheelchair closer, but Rhia wanted to sit next to Laurie on the couch. I helped Rhia sit beside her music idol and then pulled the wheelchair out of the way.

"Hello. Are you Rhia?" Laurie asked.

Rhia just grinned. I kneeled by Rhia and signed, *What's your name?*

"I'm Rhia," she said, and then she hugged Laurie.

Laurie laughed and hugged her back.

I smiled at the other Make-A-Wish mom, who smiled back. She looked exhausted, and I wondered where they had traveled from. Rhia and I had flown across the country to be in this backstage room for thirty minutes, and it was worth it, but I too was worn out. I glanced at the little girl sitting on Laurie's left and wondered what she "had." She looked healthy with dark hair and rosy cheeks, but who knows what was hidden under her skin. Cancer? Kidney failure? Heart disease? I looked at Rhia and then wondered if the other Make-A-Wish mom was also wondering what was hidden under Rhia's smile and shy giggle.

Rhia was wearing a purple beaded bracelet that she tried to pull off her wrist. I helped her take it off, and then she handed it to Laurie.

"Thank you. It's beautiful," Laurie said. She slipped it on her wrist and hugged Rhia again with tears in her eyes that she was trying to hide.

How hard this must be, I thought. *She's probably met hundreds of disabled and sick kids. Did she know this would be part of her job when she sold her first record?*

After photos were taken and more hugs were given, we were invited to join a party celebrating Laurie Berkner's new album. We stayed long enough for me to have a glass of champagne and Rhia to eat two chocolate-covered strawberries, but Rhia was exhausted, and I knew pushing her energy would be a mistake. We returned to our hotel, and after we ate an early room service dinner, Rhia fell asleep. I spent another evening staring out the window at Manhattan from fifteen stories above the city streets.

The city really doesn't go to sleep.

We had one more day to explore New York, and by then Rhia was feeling braver. We walked several blocks to Broadway, then up to Times Square and back to Rockefeller Center. We spent more than an hour inside the Disney Store on 57th Street, which is three stories high and filled to the brim with as much Disney magic as the theme park. After we returned to our room, even I fell asleep immediately after dinner.

I will never forget how Rhia looked when she saw Laurie Berkner walk on stage and play her guitar. I don't know how much she actually heard, but she appeared to hear the music and Laurie's voice. I'm sure she also heard the screams of the other children around her. A year later, Rhia couldn't hear Laurie's music anymore. I packed up all of her Laurie Berkner CDs and gave them to a friend's child, but we kept the DVD. Rhia still likes to watch it and sing along to the songs that she knows by heart.

I also wonder about the other little girl who sat beside Laurie that day. I hope she's doing well. And if she's not, how is her mom?

5

Every three to five years, Rhia declines physically. The pattern began when she reached what became her maximum physical potential at age ten. Then, slowly, her ataxia increased. Her hands shook more, and it became harder for her to walk. Her stamina declined while her anxiety increased. This is also when she probably began losing her hearing, although we didn't know she was going deaf until two years later. Then, after several months of fear (me) and frustration (her), the decline stopped, and we eventually learned to live with a new normal.

And then, age fourteen, Rhia went through another decline. She needed her wheelchair full time at school to accommodate increased fatigue. Her fine motor skills diminished even more, and the shaking in her hands made it harder for her to feed herself. She was also completely deaf by then. But once again, after the decline Rhia plateaued, and we all learned to live with that new normal. She regained a little strength, but she needed more help dressing. Weighted utensils helped her feed herself. Hearing aids were started and then dropped.

So when she started another decline at age seventeen, Rick and I were used to the cycle. I took scrupulous notes about her energy, her calorie intake, her ataxia, her menstrual cycle, and her mood, all in the hope I'd gather enough information for the doctors to understand what was happening and find a way to help her. But this time, her physical decline didn't stop after a few months. Instead, the decline escalated. Rhia slept more, missed school, and ate less. She became so lethargic she stopped walking and asked for her wheelchair at home just to go to the bathroom. She coughed every time she swallowed water. And then came the day I couldn't wake her up. Her breathing was regular and her heart sounded strong, but she was too tired to open her eyes for more than a moment. When they did open, her eyes rolled upwards into the back of her head, as if trying to see inside her own skull. It looked like a seizure.

After a frantic call to Dr. Graham's office, I called Rick. He rushed home from work and then carried Rhia to the car. I didn't wait for a return call from the doctor; I drove us all to the emergency room at Stanford. The attending doctor took one look at her lethargy, rolling eyes, and general lack of response and agreed she looked like she was having a seizure. Blood work was ordered and then an MRI and a CT scan to look for tumors. Once those were done, the neurologist on call ordered that Rhia be monitored for seizures.

On her first night in the hospital, Rhia sat up in a hospital bed and cried as a nurse attached electrodes to Rhia's scalp. I tried to distract her by playing a movie on her portable CD player, but it didn't work. Rhia was too tired to focus on the screen and too upset to be distracted. I held her hand and sang to her, even though I knew she couldn't hear my voice. When she was tiny and we had to wait at the pediatrician's office, I'd sing Rhia songs to keep her calm. Rhia would smile and sometimes sing along. Even if Rhia could have heard me that night, I doubt singing would have helped.

At last the electrodes were set and Rhia was allowed to fall asleep. She looked so tiny, and her pale skin looked whiter than the pillowcase on her hospital bed. I kept holding her hand and staring at her, willing some of my own strength to flow through my hands into hers.

The sun went down, nurses came and went. The child on the other side of the screen in Rhia's hospital room laughed as she played a game with someone. Her mom? I didn't know. We parents nodded to each other as we passed in the hall or gave a brief smile, but we tended to save our conversations for the doctors and staff.

Rick went to a hotel to get some sleep and tried convincing me I should go too, but I couldn't leave Rhia. I needed to be near her, to keep holding her hand and help her communicate with the nurses, who promised to take good care of her. I knew in my head I should go; I was already exhausted from a month of caring for Rhia during her decline. And I knew that a stay in the hospital was a marathon that required thoughtful use of one's energy. But I couldn't leave her. I remembered when she was two weeks old and got jaundice. I refused to leave then too. At least there was a chair near Rhia's bed that folded into a type of bed. I didn't have to sleep in the waiting room near the NICU this time.

There were so many children in that hospital. I walked the hallways that night, unable to sleep or sit still. Up and down the hallways, I saw room after room with two beds and a child in each one. Some of the children were alone in a room with the door closed and a sign that said, "No entry." Those were the kids fighting cancer or another disease that destroyed their immune system. Some of the children at the hospital had been there for weeks, even months. Some of them would never go home.

Rhia wore those electrodes for twenty-four hours to catch the tiniest of suspected seizures. The test showed she didn't have seizures. And there was no sign of infection or illness. She wasn't dehydrated or malnourished, but somehow Rhia was in metabolic distress, which meant her body wasn't getting the fuel it needed to function. But why? Every symptom she had pointed to a mitochondrial disease, but the mitochondrial tests had all been negative.

On the second night I finally agreed to go to the hotel with Rick and sleep. Curled up against him, I cried at last. For weeks I had kept the tears locked inside as I focused on caregiving, trying to stay strong and focused so Rhia wouldn't feel afraid. At least, that's what I told myself, when really I stayed strong to keep myself from being afraid. Now that she was in the hospital and I was in a hotel room six blocks away, my emotional walls crumbled and the tears flowed for hours.

My cell phone rang at five in the morning. Rhia was awake and needed me.

With the electrodes gone from her hair and her body slowly stabilizing with whatever they were putting in her IV drip, Rhia's fighting spirit had returned. She hugged Rick and then grabbed my hand with a strength that surprised me, as if saying, "You're not going anywhere!" Since Rhia was out of danger, at least for the moment, Rick decided to go home and back to work; he'd had as much waiting in a hospital as he could cope with and needed to be busy again. I felt relieved he went home; my crying had upset him, and he didn't know how to comfort me. Plus, his nagging at me to take care of myself was annoying.

After five days in the hospital Rhia was declared stable and out of danger, but still weak. The most worrisome impact of the decline was that she'd lost the ability to swallow correctly, which was why she coughed when she drank water. A prescription was written for speech therapy and for Thick-It, a powdered substance added to liquid that made it thicker and therefore easier to swallow. The hope was that with therapy, Rhia would regain coordinated swallowing. If she didn't, or if she lost more weight, she would need a feeding tube.

Because it was an emergency, it took only a few days for speech therapy to begin. During that time Rhia drank her thickened smoothies, still unable to eat anything solid. That changed after just one visit with the therapist. It was as if Rhia's body had forgotten how to chew food properly and then swallow, but once her body was reminded exactly what to do, her body remembered and she swallowed solid food again. Rhia started with pudding and yogurt with the therapist, working her way up to apple sauce. The first thing she ate at home with me was an avocado. I spooned the soft green avocado flesh into her mouth and watched her swallow carefully. She smiled and opened her mouth for more. She'd learned to feed herself with a spoon at age two. Here she was at age seventeen, learning to eat all over again.

"I'm like the baby in *Avocado Baby*," she said. That was one of her favorite books.

I grinned and spooned more avocado into her mouth. "You're my Avocado Baby."

She laughed, and it was the most beautiful sound in the world.

The decline was over. Now we had to figure out how to live with her brand-new, more severe symptoms. The cause was still a mystery.

6

I REMEMBER BEFORE RHIA WAS BORN HOW LONG I LAY motionless, afraid and powerless, praying that someone would save my baby. And here I was again, praying for answers, but this time my own child was the one suffering. Her body was poked and prodded, and she had zero control over when or how. I made all the decisions; she just had to go along with it. And if I didn't let the doctors do their work, I was a bad mother.

But where was the line between taking care of her body and harming her mind? I feared my constant need to understand and cure her illness was doing more harm than good.

In the autumn of 2013, we were given a tiny glimmer of hope on managing Rhia's illness. Dr. Graham called to tell me about a study of a brand-new medication that could help people with mitochondrial disease. Even though Rhia didn't have an official diagnosis, Dr. Graham was able to get her into the study. If Rick and I agreed, she could start the medicine right away.

"There will be tests to get a baseline before she starts the medication, and several more during the study," he said.

"What kind of tests?" I asked, imagining how much Rhia hated blood work.

"The usual labs. Blood and urine. She'll also need an EKG to check for any heart abnormalities. There is a slight chance the medication could cause an irregular heartbeat, so we'll need to monitor her closely."

"Are you sure this could help her?"

"I wouldn't suggest it if I didn't think there was a good chance it could help."

I trusted Dr. Graham, and I understood he had advocated for Rhia to be a part of the study. She didn't have a diagnosis, and without one she didn't meet the criteria for any trial medication or research. But somehow, Dr. Graham had got her into this one.

"Send me the paperwork and I'll talk to Rick," I said.

The paperwork arrived in a fat manila envelope three days later. Rick and I read the make-up of the experimental medicine, how the medicine supposedly worked, and what would be required of Rhia to participate in the study.

EPI-743 for Metabolism for Mitochondrial Disorders

Study Background: EPI-743 is a new drug that is based on vitamin E. Tests have shown that it can help improve the function of cells with mitochondrial problems. It may be able to treat people with genetic disorders that affect metabolism and mitochondria.

Mitochondria are the parts of cells that help produce energy. Metabolism is the process by which the body uses energy to help cells grow and reproduce. Metabolic and mitochondrial disorders affect the body's ability to produce and store energy. These disorders can cause a wide variety of problems, but most often they affect the muscles and the brain, where energy requirements are high. Treatment is difficult because the exact source of the problem is hard to detect.

Objectives:

- To see if EPI-743 can improve energy production and use in people with mitochondrial or metabolic disorders.
- Eligibility:
- Children between 2 and 18 years of age who have metabolic or mitochondrial problems.

Design:

- Participants will be screened with a physical exam and medical history. Blood and urine samples will be collected.
- The study will last about 13 months. Participants will have seven 3- to 5-day inpatient study visits about 3 months apart.
- Participants will take either EPI-743 or a placebo for the first 6 months of the study. After 6 months,

there will be a 1-month rest period. Then, those who received EPI-743 in the first 6 months will take the placebo for the next 6 months. Those who had the placebo will take EPI-743.

- During each inpatient study visit, participants will have a physical exam. A 24-hour urine collection will be obtained. Blood samples will also be taken. Imaging studies and other tests may be performed as directed by the study researchers.

Rick looked up from the paperwork and said, "That's a lot of testing. I don't think she'll put up with it."

"I don't think so either." I sighed and stared at the carefully organized stack of papers. Every page requested my initials to show that I understood the demands of the study. Did I really understand? More importantly, would Rhia understand that all those tests were meant to help her? And what if we put her through all those extra tests and it didn't help her at all?

On the other hand, what if it did?

When was the first time I held Rhia down during a blood draw while she screamed? Was she an infant? I wasn't in the room when she had jaundice at two weeks and the NICU doctor prescribed a blood transfusion. I'm sure she cried, but did she scream? I think the first time I had to force her to comply with an unwanted medical procedure was when she got her baby shots. I remember holding onto her furious baby body as the needle punctured her pale skin and then soothing her when it was done. Every parent knows that moment—listening to your baby's sobs and the unspoken, *Why are you doing this to me?*

And every parent will hold their unwilling child in the doctor's office several times in the child's life. Eventually that awful task will end; children grow and gain more understanding, and that understanding leads to acceptance. Shots keep you healthy. Blood work hurts, but it's important. When it's over, Mom will take you for ice cream.

Rhia never gained that understanding. She called blood work "blood shots" and physically fought every single one. When Rhia was little, I would sit in the chair in the phlebotomy station, put Rhia on my lap, wrap both of my arms around her body, swing one of my legs across both of hers, lift my chin out of head butting range, and then say, "Ready." Rhia screamed and jerked her whole body trying to get free of my grip. When she got older and stronger, Rick took over as human restraint while I held onto her arm to keep it steady for the phlebotomist. Every muscle in that arm tightened as she struggled to pull away. Despite all of her neurologic challenges, she has always been strong.

The fighting became a real problem when Rhia turned twelve and refused to get out of the car. I could no longer just pick her up and force her into her wheelchair. Twice she missed important labs because she had wrapped her arms around her body and the car's seat belt, turned her face away from me, and screamed, "No!" Even Rick had trouble dragging her out of the car.

We had worked with both a behaviorist and a psychologist since Rhia was six years old to help her stay calm during medical tests, but nothing had worked. With their guidance, Rick and I tried various strategies, from simple counting to ten and deep breathing techniques to, finally, spending sprees at the Disney Store. Often, nurses or technicians would try to calm Rhia down with the promise of a sticker or soothing words. They all got kicked for their efforts.

The worst was when Rhia needed a new MRI for Dr. Sanderson when she was thirteen. Since she had to be sedated, the audiologist also requested an audiogram on the same day to learn more about the way Rhia's brain processed sound. It was difficult to get an accurate assessment of Rhia's hearing with a standard hearing test, and she wouldn't sit still for the electrodes to read the signal in her neurons, so sedation made the most sense. Get two big tests done on one day so she only had to be sedated once. It was an excellent plan.

I had asked the anesthesiologist if I could give Rhia a Xanax in the morning so I could get her out of the car, but he said no. Instead, Rick and I both forcibly dragged her out of the car; it must have looked like a kidnapping. Then he carried her to the front door of the hospital before she agreed to sit in her wheelchair. In pre-op, Rhia refused to put on a gown, so I told the nurse to give her the medicine first. The nurse returned with the medication to make Rhia drowsy and forget the entire awful day. Two more nurses joined us, one who looked like she was still in nursing school. All three approached the gurney where Rhia and I sat, and then the eldest of the three said to Rhia, "Drink this, sweetie. It will make you feel better." Rhia turned away with both arms wrapped around her body and screamed, "No!"

All three nurses looked at me as if asking what to do.

I said, "Rhia, the sooner you drink it, the sooner we can go home."

Rhia screamed into my face, "I won't do it!"

"We're not leaving until you drink it." Rhia didn't get her stubbornness out of thin air.

The eldest nurse took her cue from me. "It's time to drink your medicine like a big girl." She leaned down to help Rhia drink.

Rhia whirled toward her and punched her in the face.

It was impressive how quickly the second nurse grabbed the plastic cup of medication before it spilled.

I grabbed Rhia's arms, flung both of my legs over her, and told the nurses, "It won't get any easier, so just do it."

All three nurses froze. Even Rick looked uncertain.

"Help me!" I ordered.

The youngest nurse burst into tears and left the room.

Rick grabbed Rhia's head to keep her from turning away, and the nurse Rhia punched took back the cup. As carefully as possible she dripped medication into Rhia's mouth. Rhia swallowed in between screams and coughs, then slowly began to relax. I took the cup from the nurse and helped Rhia take little sips, cooing to her in a sing-song voice, "It's okay, my darling girl. Mama's got you. It's okay . . ." I would have signed but I didn't have a free hand.

At last Rhia drifted into sleep, and I was able to undress her and get her into her gown. The nurse who had helped us handed me a warm blanket, and I tucked Rhia in. I said, "I'm sorry you got punched."

She smiled. "I've been hit harder. But your daughter is surprisingly strong."

"Do other kids fight that hard?"

"Sometimes." She put her hand on my shoulder. "You did good. It isn't easy holding your child down like that. You kept your head and stayed calm."

I stroked Rhia's sweaty forehead as she slept. "I didn't feel calm."

"I know." She looked toward Rick, who was sitting in a chair staring at the wall, then looked back at me. "You're good parents."

When Rhia was wheeled to the MRI, Rick and I went outside, shaking, both in tears and feeling like we'd tortured our only child.

Rick said, "Next time, give her the Xanax. I don't care what the doctor says."

I carried every moment that had contributed to Rhia's extreme panic during medical procedures because I was always the one choosing between Rhia's mental health or physical health. Rick and I discussed the pros and cons, and Laurent added his opinion, but ultimately it was up to me. So I had to weigh, case by case, which was the most important. Mental stability? Physical well-being?

I could only choose one for my daughter.

"Dr. Graham seems pretty convinced this medication could help," Rick said.

"We should do it," I said calmly. "We have to try. And he said that if we think it's causing more harm than good, we can stop."

Rick slid the signature pages toward me. "I agree."

I picked up a black pen with a shaky hand and scrawled my signature on the permission page.

7

After I signed the paperwork for the EPI-743 trial, we had a few weeks to wait for the first round of labs. That's when I began doubting the decision. Would the extra tests needed for the study traumatize Rhia more than the possible healing benefits of the medication? I needed reassurance that I'd made the right choice, so a friend recommended I talk to her psychic.

"She's amazing!" my friend gushed. "She helped me when I was getting a divorce and then later when I had to make a decision about my job. And she's legit. She's helped thousands of people all over the country and she's in Ukiah next week. Isn't that perfect timing?"

"A psychic? Come on . . ."

"I thought you believed in psychics." My friend sounded hurt.

"I believe people can be extremely intuitive and that can look like mind reading, but it's not magic."

"I'm telling you, this woman is the real thing. She saw things about me no one could know, and then she helped guide me on a path that felt right for me. It changed my life."

My friend leaned forward, looking so earnest with her wide eyes. I knew she'd been through hell the last few years, and somehow seeing a psychic had helped her. She clearly wanted to help me, but I doubted a psychic would ease the fear I carried around in my gut all day, every day.

"Why not," I said, more for my friend than because I thought a psychic would help. "She can't hurt."

My friend smiled and wrote down the number on a Post-it note. "She has family here, so she comes several times a year. I'm planning to see her again too."

I stared at the number sticking to the back of my hand, biting the sarcastic remark I was thinking. This is what it's come to: tea leaves and crystals. I'd been a pagan for years, but believed magic was more about personal intention and reconnection with the planet, not divination.

What the hell. No one else had any answers. Not the internet. Not the doctors. No one. And all I really wanted was an answer. Just one.

That night, I called the psychic.

Two days later, on a sunny afternoon, I drove fifteen minutes outside of Ukiah and then turned down a narrow, paved road that cut through a new vineyard. The trunks of each vine looked smaller than my arm, and their tiny branches looked too fragile to ever hold heavy bunches of wine grapes. I pulled into a new subdivision of stucco houses and parked in front of a house with the address the psychic had given me. The place looked like any other beige, garage-in-the-front, suburban house, and the woman who opened the door looked like an ordinary middle-aged mom. But according to my friend, this ordinary mom was psychic.

Her name was Rose. Shorter than I, she had long, gray-blond hair and pale blue eyes. She wore a knee-length white dress with a red-rose print that billowed around her as she walked. Her smile was brilliant with perfectly white teeth. She led me to a side room near the front door that contained two blue couches facing each other. I sat on the one under the sunny window and she sat across from me.

"How can I help?" she asked after offering me a glass of water from the pitcher on the low table between us.

"I don't really know if you can," I said, hoping my voice didn't show my skepticism. "But my friend said you were good."

"On the phone you mentioned your daughter is having a medical procedure."

"She's part of a Stanford study."

"You're concerned it might be harmful." It wasn't a question; she said this calmly while looking directly at me.

For a moment I wondered if she'd read my mind but then I realized it was fairly obvious why I was there. Sick child plus medical procedure equals scared mom.

I took a deep breath and decided to plunge in. "Rhia was born with a medical condition no one can figure out. It's degenerative, but her doctor thinks this experimental medicine could help her. I'm hopeful, but I'm scared it could be bad, and I don't know if the study is a good idea at all."

Rose touched the heart-shaped pendant on her necklace. "I can feel how difficult this decision is."

Again, I had to bite my tongue and not roll my eyes. What was it about this soft-spoken woman in the floral dress that made me want to laugh at her? I suppose it was more the idea of her as a psychic. Maybe I was actually laughing at myself for paying a stranger one hundred dollars to tell me what was going to happen to my daughter.

"You want to know why this is happening to your daughter," she said softly.

The way she said "why this is happening" made my throat tighten. I nodded, feeling tears in my eyes and forcing them to stay where they were. *Don't cry yet. You don't know this woman!*

"Let's begin," she said, closing her eyes. She folded her hands in her lap and sat up straighter, taking several deep breaths. I wasn't sure if I should do the same thing but I felt my own body relax as I watched her. The room was very still; all I heard was Rose's breathing and several birds chirping outside. It felt good to simply sit with her, whether or not she really was psychic.

"You are surrounded with darkness," she said. "So much darkness pressing down on you from every direction. Some of this darkness is yours and some has been passed down to you. That darkness is trying to touch your child."

You didn't have to be a psychic to know things were dark, but I still shivered involuntarily, suddenly feeling the weight of Rhia's disability and all of the decisions I was forced to make to keep her safe.

She smiled. "But there is great strength in you. That strength has also been passed down from your mother and is now also a part of your daughter. As much as the darkness wants your child, her strength keeps it away. Trust her strength."

Rose sat quietly again and I waited for her to say more. Just as I began wondering if she was done, Rose said, "You and your daughter are on the same path. You need each other to finish this cosmic journey. Without each other, you'll never find peace. Death is only a part of that journey. You've been reborn to each other several times." She frowned. "There is an energy that doesn't want you two to continue on your path. There is a person in your life who wants to disrupt the journey. A woman. She is jealous. Be careful around her."

Oh great, I thought. *Now I have to worry about a mysterious woman!* I wondered who that person could be or if she even existed.

Rose smiled again. "Don't be afraid. The medicine will work. Your child's strength will win the day." She opened her eyes and looked at me. "That's all I see."

The room was completely silent. Even the birds outside had stopped chirping, and the sunlight had slowly moved from the window. I waited, wondering what to do while Rose continued to look at me. Finally she asked, "Do you have any questions?"

Oh, only a million, I thought. Like . . . does Rhia really have mitochondrial disease? Is she going to die? If it isn't mito, what is it? Why is this happening to her? What can I do to help her? What is the cure? Is there a cure? Will we ever know?

"Am I doing the right thing?" I whispered, letting the tears fall.

"You are the best mother your daughter could ever have. She chose you to guide her during this lifetime. Of all the beings in the universe, you're the one she wants to be with. Have faith in that. Have faith in her."

I took a deep breath, feeling the weight of Rhia's illness lighten in my body ever so slightly. Perhaps that was the reason people talk to psychics when no one can answer their questions. All those late nights on the internet researching possible causes of Rhia's illness never gave me relief. Doctors offered ideas, but they never had an answer. Therapists brought up more questions, and ministers talked about "mysterious ways." If a crystal ball or a tarot card could bring a tiny bit of comfort, why should I push that comfort away?

8

The psychic was wrong about the EPI trial; the medication didn't work. After three months of adding the liquid into her yogurt every evening without her noticing and extra trips to Stanford for mandatory EKGs and several blood draws, her labs showed no change. The dose was increased but her lactate levels remained too high, and there were no obvious improvements in her physical symptoms. The only thing that changed was Rhia's stress level. She screamed while we dragged her to the car and then she cried as soon as she was buckled in. The three-hour drives every few weeks for a full day of studies at Stanford became unbearable for us all. Finally Rick and I decided it was time to stop. Dr. Graham agreed.

Doctors are terrible at informing parents their child has a life-threatening disease. They'll read the results of a test or check their notes from a prior exam, make an announcement about something alarming, and then leave the room.

Here are some examples of what I've been told:

"There is degeneration of her cerebellum . . ."

"I suspect ataxia telangiectasia, which unfortunately is a degenerative condition impacting motor skills and other functions. Many people with this condition have a reduced life expectancy, but this varies widely depending on the patient."

"Every indication is that your daughter may not reach her teens. But we don't know for certain."

"She may not live to age twenty, but we'll need to see how her symptoms progress over time."

"Mitochondrial disease can reduce life expectancy, but not in every case."

After the doctor leaves the room, frightened parents turn to the only expert in the room, the doctor's assistant, who is often a nurse practitioner or medical student, and nine times out of ten a woman. She will fill in the details on the bad news without saying anything specific because only the doctor can say the prognosis.

The EPI trial had ended two months earlier, and we were once again sitting in a doctor's examining room. Rhia was bored and I was in shock. Dr. Graham, whom I had trusted with Rhia's care for eight years, had just said the words, "There's nothing more we can do to stop future declines."

I glanced at Rhia, who was humming to herself, something she did when she was trying to patiently wait. "What do we do now?" I asked.

Dr. Graham said, "We wait. There is more research all the time, and one of those studies could help us determine the cause of the degeneration. But for now, we just have to wait."

Then he hugged me and I felt the compassion pour from his arms. This was why I trusted him so much; he was a doctor who had watched hundreds of patients die but never lost his compassion, and he always admitted when he didn't know something. If he was out of ideas, then there really was nothing more to do.

He stepped back and said, "You are a great mom and caregiver. Remember that." And then he left.

I turned to the only expert left in the room, a tall blond woman in a white coat named Alicia. "Did he just say Rhia is dying?"

She looked me in the eye like she was daring herself not to blink. "He is concerned by some of the test results and the overall rate of decline. He is also frustrated that he can't find a clear diagnosis despite all the available research."

"He's been concerned for years. Why is this different?"

"There are more tests available now than before so we have more information."

"And that information makes the doctor think Rhia is dying?"

Alicia kept her back straight and her eyes on mine. Her voice didn't waver; she'd obviously had this conversation before. She said, "The research gave us more understanding of how her illness is progressing."

"How is it progressing?" Rhia was humming louder to indicate her increased boredom, but I didn't look away from Alicia.

"Dr. Graham will explain everything in his written report. You should have an electronic copy tomorrow."

I whispered, "Is Rhia dying?"

Alicia blinked. Her whole body relaxed as she quietly said, "We don't know, but the loss of motor skills and increased fatigue is worrisome."

"How long does she have?"

"We can't determine an exact time frame."

"Will she make it to twenty?"

Alicia glanced at Rhia and took a deep breath. "It's possible she won't."

Rhia said loudly, "Can we go home? I'm bored of sitting here."

I smiled at her and signed, "Yeah, we're done. Let's go."

Rhia unlocked the brakes on her wheelchair and wheeled toward the door. "Finally!"

When we got to the parking lot, I saw that my car alarm had gone off. How long had it been beeping? In a strange way it was comforting, as if my car could feel my terror and was screaming.

I drove home on automatic, thinking about all the times I thought Rhia would die. First to jaundice when she was two weeks old. Then when we thought she had a brain tumor when she was two years old. At age ten we thought we'd found a diagnosis: ataxia telangiectasia. It was an answer, but also a death sentence. Then we discovered that wasn't the cause either; the death sentence was lifted, but the mystery remained. Every year there were more questions and fewer answers. Every birthday came with cake and ice cream and balloons and a tiny whisper from death: This could be her last birthday.

Seventeen birthdays had passed. If the doctor was right, Rhia only had two more birthdays left.

After Dr. Graham told me Rhia was dying, I made plans. She would be buried, not cremated, because she had fought so hard to stay on this earth. Her brain would be donated to her doctors at Stanford University, which would be a great help to others. Rhia loves helping people. We would have a celebration in her favorite park, the one she liked to walk the dog in. And then when she was buried and all of her things given away to other children, I would drive far out into the forest, park my car, hike deep into the redwoods, and disappear.

Love

"I'm so lucky! Everybody loves me!"

—Rhia, age 16

1

PEOPLE OFTEN ASK ME HOW I MANAGE TO HAUL RHIA TO so many appointments and deal with so much stress every day.

"It must be awful," someone will say.

"How do you keep from crying?" another person might ask.

It is awful and I want to cry every time, but I can't. I have to hold it together for Rhia; if I get upset, it will make the situation worse for her.

I go numb the moment I park the car in the lot near her doctor's office and then shut off the engine. I focus on what must be done, not on how much Rhia yells or how anxious I feel. My senses heighten, ready for battle. Every procedure is a battle with Rhia (get out of the car!) and with myself (don't cry!). Sometimes it is a battle with the doctor's office, the hospital, Rhia's insurance, and her social worker. Paperwork gets lost, forms aren't signed, labs are backed up, and the one important person a nurse needs to speak to won't answer the phone. While Rhia screams and fights with clenched fists, I fight with persistence and disassociation. During a procedure, like the day Rhia punched a nurse during pre-op, I am calm, focused, and in absolute control of my emotions. Nurses listen to me and even doctors pay attention. I don't yell and I am always polite. I transform into a general confidently ordering her troops into battle.

I fall apart when it's over. About an hour after we leave the doctor and are on our way home, I feel a tremble in my core, as if every tear and scream I kept shut down throughout the appointment is ready to erupt. Because I'm driving, I allow only a few tears to fall. The rest must wait until I'm home. When Rhia is settled into her own bed for sleep, I curl up in mine and cry, shaking all over. In the morning I feel tired, and it will take me a few days to feel centered again.

I've been staying strong by going numb so long it's become easy for me to shut down and disassociate when I'm afraid about Rhia's medical needs. It's also becoming harder for me to feel my own body and emotions again when the stress is over. Numbness has become normal, and I'm sure that's not a good thing. I've also noticed that when I'm in the middle of a crisis, any ordinary depression I might feel vanishes. I know exactly what to do when life is hard. When Rhia is thriving and the garden is growing and there's still money in the bank after all the bills have been paid, I have no idea how to enjoy it. Instead, I wait for the next crisis.

When Rhia was hospitalized after her health deteriorated, it felt as if I'd been kicked in the gut so hard I couldn't breathe. Frantic can't describe the feeling. But that feeling quickly dissolved as I cared for her. The frantic feeling didn't disappear; instead, it settled into my gut, spread outward to my skin, and hid in my body's tiniest cells, where it could be easily ignored.

The weaker she became, the stronger my senses grew. I heard the tiniest sounds, like the whisper of a moving leaf or a bumble bee outside, while sitting beside Rhia's bed. I saw every detail of her skin, that her lips were dryer than the day before and how the pulse on the top of her tiny hand still beat strong. I waited and watched, marking any changes in Rhia's breathing. How many hours had she slept that day? Was it harder to wake her up in the afternoon or the morning? On occasion, the fear tingled across my skin before I could push it back, like a gnat that keeps landing on your nose but is too fast and small to drive away.

People around me fell apart, including Rick. This made it even more imperative that I stay strong because I honestly believed that others were unable to care for Rhia. I never blamed them. I knew Rhia's medical crisis was terrifying, and some people just couldn't face the idea that she might die. As others withdrew, I stopped reaching out for support, deciding it was better to just focus on Rhia's needs and ignore my own.

Despite being sick, hospitalized, run through invasive tests, and looked at by more doctors than she could comprehend, Rhia kept smiling. After yelling and complaining about a blood draw or another exam, she'd crack a joke and then laugh, making everyone around her laugh too. Where does Rhia's ability to keep laughing come from?

Rhia lives right here, right now; she doesn't worry about next month or next year. Yes, I know it's easier when you're not the person tracking down doctors, filling out forms, and planning for the long term, but she is the person who lives with the disability. I can escape it for a precious few hours or a weekend away. For her, there is no escape from ataxia and fatigue. Instead of letting that reality destroy her, she keeps fighting and laughing.

Is real strength feeling a little bit of laughter after looking for the tiniest spark of joy in what seems to be a tragedy? Or is it putting your own needs aside for the benefit of another? When I began having dizzy spells from lack of sleep and regular meals while sitting beside Rhia's bed, I realized being strong is much more complicated than just going numb. It's fine to set your feelings aside to calm your child after she's thrown up again in the middle of the night. But what happens when the crisis lasts for weeks or months and the outcome is unknown? Is it possible to disassociate for long periods of time without losing yourself? Knowing how much you can give, and what you need to do for yourself so you can continue to give, seems to be an important part of strength.

Maybe Rhia really is the stronger one. She stays present and fights with voice and body. She laughs at illness and death. She forgives quickly. She loves fully. And no matter what, she is always there for others, even when they turn away from her.

2

On a smoky, sunny morning, I drove an hour and a half north on Highway 101 to Rangjung Yeshe Gomde, a Tibetan Buddhist meditation center in Leggett, north of Ukiah. I had an appointment with Lama Tsultrim Sangpo, a Buddhist monk from Tibet who had agreed to talk to me about my daughter's illness.

I've read many books written by Buddhist teachers and philosophers, especially the teachings of Thich Nhat Hanh and Pema Chödrön. I had also practiced mindful meditation since Rhia was born. But I had never spoken with a monk or nun, let alone a Tibetan lama. As I drove the highway north, climbing ridges thick with redwood trees and oaks, I wondered what he would be like. How should I greet him? Was I appropriately dressed in my slacks and long-sleeved blouse?

The retreat center was just off the highway, tucked into hills thick with trees and wildlife. I was greeted by a man who seemed to be the caretaker, and he directed me to the retreat's center, a large kitchen and dining hall where people were preparing lunch. One woman gave me directions to Lama Tsultrim's cottage. Driving on the bumpy one-lane dirt road through the hot silence of late morning, I smelled dry grass crackling in the sun. After ten minutes I saw the cottage, a tiny building with redwood siding and small windows. The Eel River gurgled several feet below, and two jaybirds yelled at me as I parked.

The front door was opened by a man wearing rust and orange robes. He had eyeglasses pushed up on his head and a cell phone in his hand.

"Hi, I'm Terena," I said.

He nodded and said, "Come in."

I remembered to take off my shoes before entering. He nodded toward a corner of the room and told me to sit down. I didn't know if he meant sit on a chair, at the table, or on the meditation cushion. I chose the cushion, but then realized maybe it was his cushion and I was rude. I was too embarrassed to get up and change to a chair.

He handed me a piece of paper where instructions on how to use the phone were written. "Do you know what this means?"

I took the opportunity to stand and get away from the embarrassing cushion to help him. He needed to check his voicemail, but the directions were confusing and I was unfortunately no help. After a few minutes he shrugged and took the phone back. He then tried to call the interpreter because although he understood English, he wanted to make sure I understood everything he was saying. He walked outside and left me alone for a few minutes.

He definitely wasn't what I expected; instead of an elderly Tibetan monk welcoming me into his room filled with incense and bells, Lama Tsultrim was about my age. He struggled with a cell phone just like any other person would, and his room was as ordinary as any one-room cottage could be.

When he returned, the interpreter was with him. The three of us sat on meditation pillows near an altar decorated with incense, flowers, and a golden statue of the Buddha. Then he asked how he could help.

I told him about my daughter's illness and that she would eventually die. "And there's nothing I can do to help her or cure her. Watching her suffer is breaking my heart, and I can't breathe from the grief and anger I feel. I can't meditate because my mind runs around in terror, and the only thing that helps is if I stay busy. I know what I'm feeling is natural, and I'm not asking to escape suffering. I'm asking for help so I can bear the suffering and be strong to help my daughter through this."

The interpreter repeated my words in Tibetan. Lama Tsultrim nodded as he listened. Then he spoke in his native language. I had never heard Tibetan spoken before. It is a beautiful, soothing language, tonal as most Asian languages but without the same high notes and short clips of Chinese or Japanese. I couldn't understand his words, of course, but I loved listening to the low melody of his voice and felt assured by his thoughtful pauses as he responded.

He spoke about the love of a mother for her child and how powerful that is, how the bond between a child and mother is stronger than anything in the universe. He told me the depth of my grief is directly tied to that bond because I love her so much. But the time will come when I will have to let go so she can move on to her next life. However, I can help her during the process of her death and eventual rebirth by staying devoted and loving her with all my being. A mother's prayers for her child are important in helping the child go on to a fortuitous birth that will bring her closer to enlightenment. But yes, the pain is great, and I need to care for myself as much as possible.

Lama Tsultrim listened with his full attention whenever I asked a question and answered quietly. I felt that he cared deeply for me and my child (a child he's never met), and that he really wanted to help relieve my pain. When I asked for specific instructions to help me find strength, he taught me a new meditation technique. Lama Tsultrim asked me if I had a relationship with a deity, and I explained that I find strength and wonder in the natural world. He encouraged me to meditate in nature and continue working with plants. He also told me to consider if an emotion or action was "useful." He didn't use terms like "good" or "bad." He asked, "Is your anger useful?"

Later, I asked myself that question when my emotions became a whirlwind in my head, and briefly I felt the same calm I felt that afternoon sitting with Lama Tsultrim. I still felt the rage, but was getting lost in it useful? Was getting drunk with Rick every night useful? Was wanting to yell at my husband because he wasn't grieving the way I wanted him to grieve useful?

Before I left the cottage, Lama Tsultrim said, "You must not harm yourself while grieving. You must continue to care for yourself, even when your daughter is gone. It is important for both of you."

I hadn't told him I wanted to die when Rhia did, but he knew. Maybe every mother felt like dying when they lost a child. Or maybe it was written all over my tear-streaked face.

3

I HAVE BEEN ON AN ANTIDEPRESSANT SINCE RHIA WAS hospitalized in 2012. Actually, I have been on them off and on since she was two years old, but I've stayed on Escitalopram since she almost died. I have also been in therapy since then. It is impossible for any human to be chronically sleep-deprived and under constant stress for eighteen years and not completely break down without some kind of psychiatric help. Some people choose alcohol and drugs or shopping and sex. I avoided all of these forms of stress relief because Rhia needed me too much for me to become a drunk shoe hoarder.

I wasn't immune, though. My grief followed me everywhere I went like a yowling black cat. It sucked my energy all day and became even stronger when I went to bed. As soon as I lay down and turned off the light to try to sleep, grief overwhelmed me and poured out of my soul through primal weeping. I couldn't stop it. My entire body shook from the strength of a mother's despair as I wailed, "Why?"

Rick tried calming me by holding my hand or patting my back and saying, "It's alright. Rhia is fine." It's hard to speak soothing words when you don't believe them, and Rick and

I both knew he was lying every time he said, "Everything will be okay."

Pinned to my bed, nothing but absolute exhaustion stopped my weeping.

When trying to comfort me didn't work, Rick started begging me to stop crying.

"I'm scared too, and your crying is making it worse," he said.

I tried to stop, but my body wouldn't. Taking deep breaths I willed my tears to cease. It didn't work.

After weeks of this, Rick became exasperated. "I can't stand this!"

So he left me alone to cry.

Why couldn't he just be with me? Why was it so important to him to make me stop crying? I needed him to sit beside me and let me weep until I stopped. That's all. No promises of everything being okay or pats on the back. I wanted compassion from my husband. Instead, he walked away.

I knew he went outside to drink wine where he couldn't hear my sobs.

The gray, silent wall between us grew so high we couldn't see each other anymore. We were no longer married people who loved each other. We had become resentful housemates caring for our dying daughter.

Finally, I went to my doctor and she put me on the antidepressant I have been on ever since. The crying spells slowly became less overwhelming, until I could cry without hyperventilating. She also prescribed therapy, but because I knew what the problem was and there wasn't any cure, I didn't think I needed to go. I told my doctor I would, but I didn't call any of the therapists she recommended.

One day, I stood in the kitchen and picked out the knife I would use when I walked into the woods after Rhia died. A thin, long, very sharp Japanese knife with a black handle that discreetly fit in my best black purse. Not the giant chef knife someone would notice missing, but a smaller utility knife.

The grief would end, I decided. I would be strong for Rhia as long as she needed me, and then I could stop.

4

"Have you thought about the DNR form?" Marti from hospice asked. She said this gently while leaning toward me. Her blue eyes brimmed with kindness. In her lap was a red form that seemed even brighter against her black skirt. I had to remind myself what DNR meant. Do Not Resuscitate. Do not intervene if Rhia is dying.

I nodded. Of course I'd been thinking about it. How could I not? I saw the end of Rhia's life as clearly as I saw Marti sitting across from me in my living room, waiting for me to plan how to take care of Rhia's body.

Rick refused to help plan her death.

"We'll deal with it when it happens," he said. "Why are you thinking about it now?"

"Because I can't stop thinking about it. I want to make decisions today when I can think and not when we're in the middle of her death."

He poured himself a glass of wine and walked toward the back door. "I don't want to talk about it."

"You never want to talk about it," I yelled as he walked out the door, letting it slam shut behind him. I didn't follow. I just gripped the edge of the cabinet and fought for control of my anger. There was no point in going after him. Why is it so easy for men to walk away? Even Rhia's biological father buried himself in work and only visited when it was convenient for him. Is it easier to distance yourself from the suffering of your child because you didn't share the close physical bond like mothers? Or perhaps it was actually harder for her dads to tolerate suffering. Maybe it was so unbearable for them they had to focus on something they could control, like work or cleaning the backyard or choosing another bottle of wine.

I sat at the kitchen table and read over the paperwork from palliative care, including the do-not-resuscitate form. I would do what needed to be done for Rhia on my own.

Palliative care was a new medical specialty in 2016, and we were lucky a small town like Ukiah had a provider. A palliative doctor was a specialist who cared for patients who were suffering from an incurable illness but they weren't dying, at least not quickly. Patients with multiple sclerosis, Parkinson's, and mitochondrial disease needed that type of ongoing, specialized care and pain management.

Rhia had been referred to hospice by her primary doctor because they had a newly established palliative care program to coordinate the medical support Rhia needed. She wasn't close to death at that time, but when she did show signs of a major decline she could be quickly transferred from palliative to the hospice program for end-of-life care. One of the decisions I needed to make for Rhia was how much intervention she would have in case of a medical crisis. If she stopped breathing, would I allow CPR? If so, at what point should CPR stop? What if she got to the hospital but needed a breathing tube to survive? Or a feeding tube? Would I even want her to go to the hospital? Should I let her die at home?

These decisions were necessary but felt impossible to make; how can any parent make them for their child?

Marti reminded me of Diane, the woman who had helped me when Rhia was a toddler. Both women were tall with short brown hair, and they both spoke with low, soothing voices. When I spoke to them, I felt that they heard and understood me rather than just nodding their heads to look sympathetic. Diane had asked what I dreamed of for my daughter; she helped me think about a possible future for Rhia in spite of the fear I was feeling. Marti was now asking me about a different future: Where and how would Rhia's life end?

I wiped tears from my cheeks and said, "Do not resuscitate."

Rhia would hate having breathing tubes and feeding tubes and machines keeping her alive. She would hate being shut away in a hospital room surrounded by people she didn't know. Rhia would want to be at home in her own bed surrounded by familiar people and the dolls she had played with since she was four.

I continued, "If she is injured and needs CPR or short-term assistance, the medical team can intervene. But if she doesn't respond and the next level is hospitalization with machines . . . she wouldn't want that."

Marti made notes as I spoke. She looked up and said, "That makes absolute sense, and it is what most people in the hospice program prefer." She showed the notes she had made on the DNR form and the boxes she had checked. "If this looks correct, sign the bottom."

After I signed the red form, she said she would fax it to Rhia's doctor and to the County Hospital so everyone had the same information and there would be no question about the decisions I had made.

Marti returned the following week to help me plan Rhia's funeral. I decided on burial rather than cremation, but first her brain would be donated to Stanford so that Dr. Graham could continue his research. Being helpful was important to Rhia, and she'd be happy knowing she could help others.

Marti checked the appropriate boxes and wrote my answers to her questions on the corresponding lines on the forms. When we were finished planning, she handed me the documents to sign.

I laughed when I signed the last form. "Some people get to help their child plan for college. I get to help my daughter plan her funeral."

"It really isn't fair," Marti said quietly.

Wiping my tears one more time, I said, "At least it's done now. I don't have to think about it anymore. When the time comes, we're ready."

"Now you can concentrate on living. There are no more treatments to look for and no more plans to be made. You can focus on Rhia's quality of life. She can do the things that make her happy and not worry about anything else."

"It feels like I'm giving up."

Marti waited until I raised my head again to look at her, then she said, "You are not giving up on Rhia. Not for a second."

I looked away and nodded, unable to speak.

"What you are doing right now takes strength and love. You are thinking about Rhia's needs and what she wants and putting those first."

I still couldn't look at her when I whispered, "I'm afraid I'm not strong enough to do this."

"You are," Marti said. "And you will not do it alone."

I laughed and looked back at her. "Yes, I will. Do you see anyone else in this room?" I thought about Rick hiding at work and my mother who cried too much and my dad who tried to make everyone laugh and Rhia's bio-dad who only came to visit every few months. I thought of my niece Lindsay and her mom Margie exploring colleges two years before high school graduation. I felt that I was the only person in Rhia's life willing to stand beside her all the way to the end. I felt utterly alone.

Marti read my mind. "I know you feel alone. I felt alone too when my child died."

I must have stared at her too long, but Marti just sat there looking at me with a small, sad smile. "I'm so sorry," I finally said.

"She was ten," Marti said. "That was twelve years ago."

"Is that why you work for hospice?"

"Yes. I was already a social worker, but after two years, once I was ready to work again, I decided I wanted to help other families going through what I did."

"How long did it take to . . .?"

"To feel human again?"

I nodded, unable to speak because of the tears in my throat.

"A year to feel like the world wasn't upside down. Another year to laugh again. And every year since then to learn to live with the missing of her. She wanted to be a teacher when she grew up and help people, so I'm helping people now for her."

"What was her name?" I asked, trying to smile.

Marti smiled brightly. "Maria."

I wondered how she could smile like that after losing her child. "That's a pretty name," I said.

We sat quietly together, just two mothers thinking of our daughters in my peaceful living room.

5

Families of children with disabilities and chronic illness have been the greatest support to me. We are not bound by governmental regulations and implied gag orders, meaning we tell each other everything about how to get services for our kids when programs try to hide information. We speak openly and freely about our fears and what pisses us off. When our children reach the tiniest milestone, something as simple as holding a cup with one hand for a whole minute, we celebrate together as if that child just scored the winning point for their school's soccer team. No one comprehends the hours of hard work it took for that child to strengthen the muscles in their hand to grip a smooth sippy cup without letting it drop to the floor like the other families, parents, and caregivers of so-called special needs kids.

Rhia still didn't have a specific diagnosis of mitochondrial disease, but I soon discovered not having a diagnosis is very common. Even today as I write these words, there are still more questions than answers in mitochondrial research.

It was another parent who introduced me to the United Mitochondrial Disease Foundation. Her name was Norma and she also lived in Ukiah. Her daughter Heidi had died in her late twenties, and Norma coped by working for UMDF as a parent liaison and the coordinator of the Bay Area Walk-A-Thon. Even though we lived in the same town, she wasn't someone I would have met. She was conservative and a Republican. I was, and still am, a progressive Independent. Our ideologies were miles apart, but the love of our mito children brought us together.

Politics become unimportant when your child is ill; who cares how you vote when you're fighting for the survival of your child? Norma showed me a large, international community of parents, patients, researchers, and medical specialists. Then she encouraged Rhia and me to join her at the National United Mitochondrial Disease Foundation conference, which was in Seattle that year.

Rhia was excited to fly on an airplane, stay in a hotel, and meet more kids "like her." She was the only person she knew who used a wheelchair and had ataxia. Norma met us that evening for the opening reception dinner and introduced us to almost everyone. I'm serious when I say "everyone." Norma was clearly the unofficial greeter of the UMDF. With her red-blond hair pulled up into a bun and her sparkly white blouse, she smiled warmly, reached out to strangers, shook hands, told jokes, hugged those she remembered from last year's conference, and by the end of that one evening had made ten new friends. It was as if Norma's love for her daughter had only grown since Heidi's death and because that love had nowhere to go, Norma gave it to everyone who needed it.

The next day Norma introduced Rhia and me to the coordinator for the Teen/Young Adults group. The conference had separate social activities for mitochondrial disease patients between ages sixteen and twenty-two. There was a daily support group, private meetings with specialists, group activities, fun outings, and finally a fancy ball on the last night of the conference. These were opportunities for young people to talk openly about their struggles without parents involved, but because Rhia needed me to interpret I had to be there.

I did my best to only act as Rhia's interpreter rather than as her mom by only looking at Rhia and interpreting what a person said without showing any reaction to it. I kept my body turned toward Rhia. The other members of the youth group appeared to accept my presence as an interpreter, and if anyone felt uncomfortable having a parent in the room they didn't show it. Each person spoke openly about how hard it was to manage mitochondrial symptoms while in school, how they had to limit their activities due to poor stamina. One girl talked about having to switch to her power chair full time and how grateful she was that her friends didn't treat her any differently. In fact, it was easier for her to go to the shopping mall with them now. Another girl said she was afraid to go to college because she didn't know if she could keep up with her classes. She wanted to be a nurse but didn't think she could. When she cried, the young man sitting beside her held her hand. There were stories about medication and side effects that made everyone laugh. There were complaints about overprotective parents and a few stories about annoying doctors. The support group lasted for two hours, and during that time I think I got more out of it than Rhia. The participants were typically developing young adults with a medical condition that limited their abilities, but they were not developmentally delayed like Rhia. Most of what they talked about went over Rhia's head. When the facilitator encouraged her to talk, Rhia talked about Disneyland.

There was one young man who took an interest in Rhia. At the end of the support group, he introduced himself to us and asked if he could push her chair to the conference room where lunch was being served. He sat next to Rhia, and when she dropped her napkin he picked it up. He talked to her but only asked me to interpret when I finished my meal. Later, we all went back upstairs to attend a chat about companion dogs. I stepped back and let him push her wheelchair and introduce her to his friends.

The next day he waited for Rhia near the door of the conference room and then wheeled her to the next activity, a robotics race. They worked together building a race car and then raced it against other people, him holding the remote control while she pressed the button. He rarely needed me to repeat what she said in her breathy, ataxic voice, and he instinctively understood how to hold an object so she could see it as well as interact with it.

"You've been very helpful making Rhia feel included. She didn't quite fit in, but you helped a lot," I said when the activity ended.

He smiled. "I'm glad. It's a good group and it's helped me a lot. It's hard having mito, and nobody understands. I mean, what even is it?" As we walked to the elevator he said, "This is my last year. I'll be twenty-two in November so I'll go to the adult groups at the next conference."

"Is that a hard change?"

He shrugged. "It's okay. I mean, I'm glad I'm an adult, you know? The doctors didn't think I'd live this long. I'm just happy I did!"

The elevator doors opened. As we rode together to our respective floors, he talked about the dance party that night and hoped Rhia would come. But when the dance started at eight, Rhia was exhausted and fast asleep in bed.

I've attended three UMDF conferences since then, two in Washington, DC, and one in Nashville, but Rhia has only been to the one in Seattle. I found it too exhausting to be her caregiver and interpreter and still try to keep up with all the activities for both youth and parents. She hasn't asked to go back, so I don't feel too guilty going on my own.

When I went to the conference the next year in Washington, DC, I looked for the young man who'd been so kind to Rhia.

He wasn't there. Neither were his parents.

I don't know if he's still alive.

6

Several days after Rhia's last appointment with Dr. Graham, Rick announced that Rhia needed to be baptized. "It's important to my family," he said. "And if Rhia dies without baptism my family will never forgive me."

Rick comes from a large, Southern, devoutly Lutheran family. In fact, his ancestors helped establish the Lutheran church in New Orleans a hundred and fifty years ago. When he left Louisiana, Rick also left the church, so I was surprised when he talked about baptizing Rhia.

"Why won't your family forgive you?" I asked.

"If she isn't baptized she won't go to heaven."

I stared at him, not understanding what he was saying. Finally I said, "Are you telling me that your family believes that if Rhia isn't baptized she'll go to hell?"

He nodded with tears flooding his eyes.

I didn't know if what he said about his family's beliefs was true, but I understood that he believed it was true, which added to his grief. So I agreed to baptism for Rhia.

At first, Rick tried having her baptized Lutheran but there were too many rules preventing that. The Lutheran church required that I too be baptized and that Rhia's godparents be Lutheran. To be baptized, I'd first have to go to catechism and then officially join the church, which I didn't want to do. Baptists and Methodists had similar requirements. After searching on the internet, I found the United Church of Christ and a pastor willing to baptize Rhia without requiring that we all join the church.

On a chilly March afternoon in 2012, I walked to the large, red-and-brown church on Spring Street. On the front lawn was a tall oak tree pinned with a sign that said, CAUTION. ACTIVE BEEHIVE. STAY BACK. *Even bees were allowed in this church*, I thought as I entered the front door.

A small gray-haired woman with gold glasses and a warm smile greeted me.

"Hello. I'm Pastor Cherie." She reached to shake my hand and then led me to the dining room, where she had set up two chairs for our visit.

"How can I help?" she asked as soon as we sat.

I explained about Rhia's recent near-death experience and how having Rhia baptized would help our family.

Pastor Cherie kept her blue eyes on me the entire time I spoke, nodding her head with kind compassion.

"This is an extremely difficult time for you and your family. What does Rhia think about it?" Pastor Cherie asked.

"Rhia doesn't understand what's going on. She's just happy the doctor stopped dragging her into appointments or taking her blood."

"Rhia doesn't understand her illness?"

"No. Rhia lives in the moment. She knows her body has changed, and it makes her mad, but she's never asked about what's going to happen. She doesn't understand death."

"Have you thought about what to say to her if she asks?"

"All the time! But what do I say to a girl like Rhia who's developmentally delayed, has an unknown degenerative disease, and doesn't know what any of that means?" I shrugged. "I guess I'll think of something when she asks me."

Cherie nodded. After a pause she asked, "What do you think will happen when she dies?"

I shrugged. "I don't know. I'd like to think there's a heaven, but it's hard to believe."

"You said on the phone that you're not religious. May I ask what you believe? Do you believe in God?"

I had to think about that for a minute. My mother was a Christian, but she didn't take us to church very often, mostly because my father was an atheist. They both encouraged my brother and me to find our own spiritual path. I became Wiccan in high school, something all Stevie Nicks–loving adolescents do. Later I found Buddhism. Christianity felt domineering, and with its worship of a cross, gruesome to me. My mother feared God, my father didn't believe in God, and I was somewhere in the middle, looking for the meaning of life but, just like a diagnosis for Rhia, never finding an answer.

Pastor Cherie leaned forward and said, "I'm not trying to grill you about faith, I'm trying to get an understanding of what you believe so I know how to help you and your daughter."

"I believe in God," I said. "But I don't believe in an old man sitting on a golden throne in the clouds."

Pastor Cherie smiled. "Neither do I."

We sat in comfortable silence for a while as I considered how to explain my belief about God to a Christian minister.

Pastor Cherie was undoubtedly a Christian, but I had the feeling I could trust her; she wouldn't judge me.

"I think God is more of a spirit than an entity," I began. "Not a he or her or they, but an energy. Something we can't explain. Something constant and real that is a part of us."

Cherie nodded. "You're right. We can't define God. We try very hard with our books and our churches, but how can anyone define the unknowable? We know that God is love, but what is love? A feeling? Love is powerful, and love is the only way we can come close to understanding God."

"Do you have to be a Christian to feel God?" I was nervous asking a pastor such a confrontational question, but I had to know what she thought. Was this woman the right person to baptize my child? "Rhia doesn't know who Jesus is."

Again Pastor Cherie smiled warmly. "No. You don't have to be a Christian, but being one helps strengthen your connection with God's love. This church"—she raised her hands upwards, indicating the space we sat in and the sanctity of the place—"follows the teachings of Christ in action and word. We focus on love, acceptance, and hope. We serve everyone, including non-believers."

Then she leaned toward me and held my gaze with her own. "We serve, but we are Christian. Your daughter's baptism will be a Christian baptism, with all the symbolism and prayers that are required. If you are comfortable with that, then I am happy to baptize Rhia."

I looked away from her and gazed around the echoing room and the high ceiling held up with redwood beams. A large wooden cross with gleaming polished wood shone in the dim sunlight that peeked through yellow-glazed windows.

Rows of empty pews waited for a congregation of people who followed a faith I didn't comprehend. But the room felt peaceful, even friendly. I felt my child would be welcomed there.

Looking back at Pastor Cherie, I smiled. "Yes. I'm comfortable with that. Thank you."

We chose a date two months later on the afternoon of June 20.

For a month I tried explaining the baptism ceremony to Rhia. The best I could do was tell her it was a celebration of how much she was loved by God and everyone she knew. She came to church a few times to meet Pastor Cherie and liked the singing but was instantly bored by the sermon, no matter how hard I tried to interpret and make it interesting for her. Afterwards we joined the congregation for coffee and cookies in the church kitchen. Everyone was charmed by Rhia, and she loved all the attention, especially from the elderly ladies, who kept passing her cookies. They told Rhia how excited they were about her baptism while I interpreted.

Rhia said, "I still don't get it!" Then she ate her cookies.

I continued attending Pastor Cherie's church to get a feel for her message and the congregation. On Sundays the large, echoing sanctuary filled with the voices of only a handful of people. The majority were older, probably in their seventies. More than half had some kind of disability. We sang songs to the accompaniment of a guitar played by a dark-haired woman in her forties. Pastor Cherie was helped during the service by another woman, who was the deacon. The church could have held two hundred people, but only twelve came every Sunday. Like most churches in the United States in the early 2000s, the United Church of Christ in Ukiah was losing members to old age and lack of faith. Two years after Rhia was baptized, the church building would be sold to an evangelical group, and the UCC would move their tiny congregation to a storefront near the Ukiah airport.

But on the day Rhia was baptized, fifty people crowded into the first five pews. Rhia's family and all of our friends came to witness the baptism, even those who didn't believe in the Christian God. My mom sat beside my brother and Margie, smiling while weeping. Rick's parents flew from Louisiana, and one of his brothers stood as godfather. Even Laurent came.

The entire church congregation came to witness Rhia's baptism, and for one beautiful day the church was filled with warmth and singing.

My father refused to come though, saying, "Anyone who thinks a beautiful, innocent girl will go to hell because she isn't baptized is full of shit. I won't be a part of it."

I tried explaining why I had agreed to the baptism, but he didn't hear me. And really, I wasn't completely sure myself.

Rhia sat in her wheelchair, wearing her best floral dress and shiny red shoes. She stared at all the people, at Pastor Cherie, and then at me. She loudly said, "I still don't know what's going on!"

A few people giggled as Rhia's words echoed through the church. Rick patted her shoulder and Pastor Cherie smiled. I suddenly felt as if I were dragging her to another hated doctor's appointment; I just kept making her do things she didn't understand and didn't want to do.

Pastor Cherie blessed Rhia with prayers before gently pouring half a cup of warm water on Rhia's head. Rhia scowled. As the deacon wiped the water off of Rhia's face, I glanced at the people watching. My mom was still crying happily. Rick's parents were smiling. Many of my friends clearly would have cheered, but we were in a church so they grinned and wiggled instead. Even Rick looked happy standing beside me with a hand on Rhia's wheelchair.

Rhia stopped scowling when we went home for the big party. She still didn't understand why she had to have water poured on her head, but she liked getting presents for doing it, which Lindsay helped her open. Rhia put a large piece of wrapping paper on Lindsay's head and laughed. The two girls giggled together while playing with the wrapping paper, clearly adoring each other's company as they leaned closer and held hands. After the gifts were all opened and the snacks devoured, Lindsay and Rick helped Rhia move to the bench swing, where the two girls sat side by side. Rhia sang a song about friendship as Lindsay used her feet to push the swing back and forth.

I sipped champagne with my friends and family while celebrating . . . what, exactly? Rhia was baptized so that the Christians in our family wouldn't suffer greater grief when Rhia died. She was now saved from something I didn't understand, and she could go to heaven when she died. God would protect her now, as if God hadn't been protecting her all along. I agreed to the baptism as an act of love to ease the suffering of others.

Maybe that's what baptism is about, I thought. *Baptism is an act of love by alleviating suffering and following a ritual that builds community. Community is what both Rhia and I need.* On that day in our own backyard, Rhia was surrounded by people who loved her, no longer isolated from her community. And maybe isolation was what Rick feared when he requested that Rhia be baptized. He knew he would lose his child, and he dreaded losing his family too.

I only feared losing Rhia and I was used to isolation, so Rhia being baptized brought me little comfort.

Why was Rhia born with a mitochondrial disease? Children are born every day with illness and disability all over the world. Why? What is the point of illness? Of disease? Of suffering? No parent should have to bury their child, but so many do. One day I would bury mine.

7

There was nothing more to be done after the baptism and the plans were made for her death. No one had any idea how long Rhia would live. The consensus was that she would never see age twenty-five. She probably had at most five more years. Once the plans for her death were completed, I stopped looking for cures. I had tried everything to save her, and now there was nothing to do but wait. Rick found solace in a bottle of wine. I found solace . . . where?

I went into the backyard to my garden. It was the end of July. The blossoms had disappeared, and soon there would be a fresh crop of apples on our tree. The garden was struggling to defend itself from earwigs and caterpillars, but inch by inch the baby squash, the cucumber plant, and the tiny tomato vines kept growing, determined to grow faster than the bugs could eat them. Their battle required my help, so I spent several minutes picking off earwigs and throwing them in a can to feed my neighbor's chickens. Then I watered each plant, ensuring they'd survive the warming afternoon sun. The plants were getting stronger. I felt my breathing slow, and the tremble in my body stopped. My teeth still hurt from clenching my jaw too tightly, and there were much bigger bags under my eyes that I suspected were permanent, but overall, I was stronger.

Working in my garden helped me regain my balance as the weeks went by. As I worked, I stayed completely focused on the tiny plants as they turned dark green in the sunshine. Taking a deep breath, I smelled the dirt as it tumbled through my bare fingers. The hummingbird who had won the feeder through a hard battle with at least four other hummingbirds zipped over my head. The jaybird who returned every spring yelled at me from his favorite perch on the back fence. Life kept thriving, and with the help of my garden I stayed present to its rhythm.

Why did Rhia have mitochondrial disease? Because disease is a part of nature, of life. There is no reason other than that she is alive and a part of the world. Despite her illness she is thriving and strong. She is herself. I needed to be as mindful to her as I was to my garden.

One day Rick picked up Rhia from school, and I heard her yelling through the back door, "Mom! What are you doing?"

Gathering strength, I thought.

I dusted off my hands and walked inside to say hello.

Staying in the moment with Rhia, discovering profoundly who she was, and accepting the limitations in her life were helping me find relief from my own suffering. I had also finally begun therapy to learn ways of coping with the exhaustion and anxiety. But the weight of her impending death was still too heavy. It clouded my ability to stay in the here and now.

Whenever I need support, I find it in books. To this day, I still love wandering the aisles in bookstores looking for answers. Sometimes I know exactly what I'm looking for, and other times I discover a question when I pick up a book I find interesting, like when I discovered a book about natural housekeeping and realized I wanted to learn how to clean everything with vinegar and salt. And the day I picked up a book called *Monsters* about monstrous men and the art they create, I discovered I was struggling with that very issue. How could I love the writings of Henry Miller when he was such a misogynist prick?

One day I found a book about anticipatory grief, and I finally understood the type of grief I was experiencing.

Anticipatory loss is also called ambiguous loss. It is grieving without closure. Family members of people with Alzheimer's know this type of loss intimately. Having a child with an unknown illness that will "probably" cause their death puts everyone who loves that child into grief purgatory. You don't know when it will end or how you'll cope; you just know that you're all stuck in a mystery that feels like you're being cut by a thousand stinging nettles every day. It hurts, but you get used to it. You watch your loved one lose a little more of themselves until they are gone, but their body is still sitting in their favorite chair.

I was learning to live with anticipatory loss. I knew Rhia's death was coming, but I had no idea when. Tomorrow? Next week? Next year? I wondered how many birthdays we would celebrate and how many trips to Disneyland we would take. It was impossible to plan for the future, so I focused on the now, just like Rhia did. Tomorrow didn't exist for either of us. Rhia lived fully in the today and I had to live there too, whether or not I wanted to.

My ability to see and be with Rhia in the here and now had become clouded by anticipatory loss. Every bruise and bump made me anticipate her demise. Every common cold made me anticipate pneumonia. I kept at least half a tank of gas in my car at all times just in case we needed to rush to the hospital. I watched her lose a little more physically and cognitively and anticipated the day she would lose it all.

There is also the ambiguous loss over the life you dreamed your child would have, as well as the life you planned for yourself. And the dreams you didn't know mattered to you. Dreams of helping your daughter heal from her first broken heart, of advising her about birth control when she turns fifteen and falls in love again, of helping her dress for the prom and waiting up late for her to come home. Ordinary events in a teenager's life. You want to worry about your daughter when she's out with her friends, not worry about how bad her ataxia might get.

But there she was, all grown up and soon to graduate high school. She wasn't going to college. She had no plans for her future, and I had no plans for mine. All I knew was she was still with me and I would be there for her as long as needed. To do that, I had to find a way to carry the grief and worry in such a way that it would no longer blind me to the joy of my life.

Grief is said to be the absence of a person or place we love. We carry the love with us even when the person is no longer in our world. A breakup is painful when the love is still there, and that love burns inside of us until the heat slowly fades. Death is devastating because the person we love has vanished, but the love remains powerful enough to remind us of them every day. We grieve the absence, but we also grieve the weight of the love we carry that we can never set down. Over time, the weight of that love will feel normal to us, as if the heaviness has always been there. Grief binds to our hair and our teeth, as ordinary a companion as our own heartbeat.

It is the love that makes grief so powerful. And it is love that gives us strength.

8

I SWITCHED MY FOCUS FROM THE WHY OR HOW OF RHIA'S disabilities and I focused on Rhia herself. When someone you love is dying, every moment with that person becomes more than precious. There is no time to wonder about the whys.

It took seventeen years for me to stop looking for answers and miracles that would save my daughter. Once I stopped imagining how I could make life easier for her or fix something about her, I saw the young woman she'd become. At eighteen she was still tiny, only five feet tall and barely ninety-five pounds. But in that tiny frame was an immense spirit. Rhia lived fully in the here and now. She laughed with her whole body, sometimes so hard she'd fall unless someone held onto her. She was kind to everyone, and even though she couldn't see or hear when someone was sad, she felt it instinctively, crossing a room to sit beside a friend and hold their hand. She never stopped singing loudly, even when she lost her hearing. Singing out of tune didn't matter.

"I sing from my heart," Rhia said.

Rhia started singing the moment she realized she had a voice. She sang before she babbled. Her high-pitched baby voice quickly grew in intensity as she learned to take a deep breath and let the air out in one long, loud burst of happy sound. By age one she incorporated babbling syllables into her tunes, creating her own songs that only other babies and maybe small birds understood. I sang to her every day, and she mimicked the tone of my voice. Her voice was beautiful. She didn't screech like other children, although she sometimes did to be funny. She sang softly to herself while playing with her toys on the floor of the living room, and I understood the intention behind her made-up songs. Her singing said, "I'm happy."

Eventually she learned other people's songs, especially the soundtracks from her favorite television shows. *Blue's Clues*, *Arthur*, *Barney*, *Sesame Street*, and *Little Bear* became the inspiration for hours of singing. Rhia only had to hear a song a few times before she memorized the words, but she learned the tune after hearing it just once.

Rhia learned more songs in school, classic songs like "She'll Be Coming 'Round the Mountain," "Oh, Susanna," and "Yankee Doodle." She particularly loved "This Land Is Your Land." She was fearless, singing with deep breaths and a wide open mouth, letting all the music she felt pour out of her lungs.

The only time Rhia stopped singing were those two years in middle school when she became officially deaf and was forced to try hearing aids. The fact that she stopped singing when she was thirteen made me more worried than the fact that she had lost her hearing. But when she transitioned to high school, she found her voice again. She threw away the hearing aids, opened her mouth, and sang just as exuberantly as ever.

But I was surprised when Rhia decided she wanted to join the high school choir her sophomore year, and even more surprised when her teacher supported the choice.

"If Rhia can't hear, how can she be in choir?" I asked her teacher. Back then, I still had a lot to learn about deaf culture and ableism. If Rhia wanted to join choir today, I would help her do it. But when Rhia was fifteen I was still trying to protect her and encourage her to do things I thought were appropriate. Choir wasn't on that list.

Her teacher, thank goodness, advocated for Rhia's decision. "Rhia has explored several electives at school and choir class is the only one she enjoyed visiting. She perked up and smiled while watching choir practice, and she clearly said she wants to be in choir."

"She didn't like art?"

"Rhia said art was boring."

I reluctantly agreed to support Rhia joining her high school's choir.

Ableism. The belief that a disabled person is unable to make decisions for herself or that she needs more help than she really does. I wanted to protect my daughter from being teased or stared at. Mostly I wanted to protect her from the pain of not being able to do something she wanted to do. But by protecting her, I denied Rhia the opportunity to try new things and test her own limits, which taught her resilience and independence. I was showing her that she couldn't be trusted to make decisions for herself or even know what she wanted for herself.

I was keeping her dependent on me.

Rhia was determined to live her own life, and joining choir was the first step. She was visually impaired, could barely walk even with the support of a walker, and had lost her hearing. She had lost more in her fifteen years than most people could imagine living without. But she absolutely refused to give up singing.

The mostly girl students in the choir immediately fell in love with Rhia, and the choir teacher did her best to accommodate. Rhia sat in her wheelchair near the risers as the choir practiced their songs. She was provided with a music stand that held the same lyric sheet all the other choir members had, even though Rhia couldn't read it. When the choir sang, Rhia grinned and often hummed along as if she were hearing the song. Perhaps she felt it. And when the song ended Rhia often cheered and clapped, making everyone smile.

Choir class was three days a week, and on Fridays many students sang solos they had practiced. Rhia sang every time, holding the microphone with both hands to keep it steady while belting out "This Little Light of Mine" as loud as she could. Everyone cheered when she was done, and Rhia blushed with pride. She loved singing in front of an audience. If she'd had the stamina, Rhia would have auditioned for the school musical just for the applause.

The only time Rhia had difficulty being included in choir was during dress rehearsal for the spring concert. The stage in the multi-purpose room didn't have a ramp, and Rhia was unable to climb stairs. Her teacher called me to troubleshoot the problem. But it was Rhia who found the solution.

"I can go upstairs! I just need help." Wheeling herself to the base of the stairs leading to the stage, she parked her wheelchair, locked the brakes, and undid her buckle. I quickly moved beside her as she reached both hands out for the metal stair rails.

"Wait," I said. I pushed her chair closer then helped her stand. With me behind her for support, Rhia climbed each step one at a time, stepping with one foot then bringing her feet together. Her teacher stood nearby as extra help in case Rhia lost her balance. One of the students grabbed a folding chair from a stack and set it beside the risers where all of the students would sing. Once we reached the stage, another student grabbed Rhia's left arm while I supported the right, and we three walked together to the chair held steady by yet another student. It took teamwork, but Rhia made it to the stage.

"See!" Rhia said triumphantly after she sat down on the metal chair. "I told you!" The choir cheered and the teacher smiled.

I held out my hand for a high five. "Well done," I said. Rhia slapped my hand and grinned.

Unfortunately, the actual concert began at seven that night and Rhia was too exhausted to attend; she was sound asleep while her classmates sang. It didn't seem to bother her, though. Rhia was prouder of climbing those stairs to reach the stage than she was worried about missing the performance. It was more important to her that she proved to herself she could climb those stairs and reach the stage than actually singing a song.

9

Rhia received a certificate of completion rather than a diploma when she graduated high school. A certificate means that she achieved her IEP goals by studying an adapted, alternative curriculum. It was still a challenging education, but not an educational path leading to a diploma. A diploma requires passing standardized exams and following a state-mandated curriculum. The curriculum can be adapted to create accessibility for a student with disabilities, but the substance of the curriculum cannot be changed. Even with one-to-one support, extra time, and accessible technology, Rhia could not meet the state-mandated standards. Her education followed an individualized set of coursework. She learned arithmetic up to grade two and reading up to grade one, but that was as far as her abilities could master. Her curriculum also included American Sign Language, social skills, orientation and mobility, basic shopping and money management, art, physical education, home economics, choir, and self-determination. She understood that she lived in the State of California and she could point to it on the map but didn't know what the other states were called. She could count out loud from one to twenty in order but didn't remember which number came after eleven without counting from one again. She counted objects but often couldn't remember how many there were so had to count them again. She knew enough to make decisions for herself and express her wishes, but she would always need help with basic life skills as an adult.

My niece graduated from high school the same year as Rhia and had been accepted to Chico State University for the fall term. She wanted to be a teacher. Once again, the old grief hit me like a blow to my heart, and I couldn't help comparing Rhia to her cousin. I wanted to look at colleges and plan for the future with my daughter. I wanted to help shop for a graduation dress and be a chaperone at the senior trip and help her fill out scholarship forms for college. I felt guilty for being envious of my sister-in-law, and I desperately wanted to stop feeling that way. Would I ever stop comparing Lindsay's success to Rhia's failure? Because that's what I was doing; Lindsay was the benchmark for everything Rhia would never achieve, and that kind of resentment was bad for everyone. It caused me pain, and it was destroying my relationship with my niece. It had to stop. I was determined to stop pushing Lindsay away for being able-bodied, and when I got the invitation to her high school graduation, I decided that would be the place to start healing.

I spent so much of my energy trying to make things "normal" for Rhia, but what I realize now is I was trying to make them normal for myself. I saw other children with disabilities participating in ordinary rituals and activities, and I was determined that Rhia would share their experience. I wanted Rhia to fit in somewhere . . . anywhere! Even after high school, it would take me several years to stop fighting the world to make it accessible for Rhia. All it did was make me sad and make her angry at me.

Rhia was fine in her small world. She was lonely sometimes and frustrated when she didn't understand something, but overall, she was happy. She didn't need graduation ceremonies to feel included or even camping trips with her cousins. She needed to feel seen and supported by those around her. She needed to know I had her back, and she needed both of her dads to hold her hand. She needed her cousin to color pictures with her. And she needed people to understand her language, ASL. I wish I could say I understood what she wanted early in her life, but Rhia gets her stubbornness from me. If I want something to happen, I'll beat myself black and blue to make it real. And if it's for my daughter, I'll beat myself bloody. The problem was that I didn't always realize when I needed to fight for her and when I was actually fighting against her.

I wanted Rhia to attend her graduation ceremony on the football field with all the other graduating students. I wanted to be one of those parents sitting on the hard metal chairs in the too-hot sun, patiently sitting through one boring speech after another, just to see their child wearing the traditional cap and gown receive their high school diploma. Or high school certificate. It didn't matter which. I wanted the ceremony, and once again, Laura did her best to make it happen.

Every week, Laura focused Rhia's orientation lessons on preparing her for the graduation ceremony. She explained to Rhia what the ceremony meant, why it was important, and even what people wore. She brought a cap and gown for Rhia to try on. And then every day for the month leading up to graduation, Rhia and her aid went out to the football field and walked around the area where the graduation ceremony would be held. But no matter how methodical the route and how much the event was explained to her, Rhia didn't understand why I wanted her to go. From her perspective, she was being asked to go out to a part of school she'd never been to that was wide open with no walls or roof, and as far as she could tell, no limits. She was then being asked to sit out there in her wheelchair for too long, not understanding what was happening, while people who didn't know ASL talked and talked and talked. She couldn't see what was happening, she couldn't hear what was happening, and she didn't understand why it was happening. Even the cap was a challenge. It kept falling off her head, and she said it was stupid.

"It doesn't even keep the sun out of my eyes!" she said.

Eventually, I agreed with Rhia. Graduation ceremonies are stupid.

We still had a graduation ceremony but not the one I dreamed of. Instead, Rick and I threw a party for Rhia at our house on graduation day, several hours before the so-called real ceremony at the high school. We invited every person who had helped Rhia achieve her high school certificate, every teacher, aid, and therapist, as well as family and close friends. Surprisingly, almost everyone came, and our tiny house was crammed with more than fifty people ready to celebrate Rhia.

Rhia decided to wear her favorite Tinker Bell shirt for her graduation rather than a dress, and she skipped a cap and gown.

She stood beside me in the living room, both hands gripping her walker, looking down at her feet with a huge smile on her face. I did my best to sign and say a speech at the same time.

"Thank you everyone for being here," I said. I pointed to Rhia. "They're here for you."

She smiled shyly and said, "That's nice." Everyone laughed.

I said to the guests, "We really appreciate you being here. And Rhia"—I turned again to Rhia and said as I signed—"everyone here is so proud of you, because you . . ." Rhia looked down and I waited for her to look at me again. It was too exciting; Rhia needed to take in all the attention in small, manageable bits.

When she glanced at the people watching and then back at me, I said, ". . . you finished school! You did it!" I held up a gold necklace with a GRADUATE medallion and placed it around her neck. "This is for you, because you're grown up and finished with school."

Rhia grinned and looked down at the shiny plastic medallion that gleamed against her Tinker Bell T-shirt. She held it with one hand, looked back at me, and said, "Yeah." She reached out to hug me, saying, "That's so nice."

People cheered again. I waited for a pause and said, "Again, thank you everyone for coming and for being such a huge support to Rhia. You all helped her reach this goal, and I cannot thank you enough for your dedication. You believed in Rhia, and I'm so glad we moved to Ukiah when she was in the second grade. Thank you! Oh, and one more thing." I looked toward Laura, the teacher who had been with Rhia the longest, from preschool in Lake County all the way to graduation in Ukiah. "Laura, you can retire now."

Everyone laughed and cheered again. Rhia gripped her medallion with one hand and reached up to hug me with the other. I held her tightly to help her keep her balance as well as from happiness. Rhia giggled, looked around the room, and then declared she was thirsty. With a snap of her walker brakes she moved away from me and toward the kitchen, party guests quickly moving to get out of her way.

Lindsay graduated high school a week later. Rhia decided to stay home with Rick, still afraid of the wide-open football field. I sat in the front row with my brother and his wife, feeling proud and determined not to let envy spoil the moment. Lindsay was beautiful despite the ugly orange cap and gown. Her long dark hair hung loose down her back, and her brilliant smile made my heart swell with joy. Here she was, all grown up, walking across the podium to accept her diploma. In a flash I saw Lindsay as a baby in my arms, a third grader playing with Rhia in the sandbox, a middle schooler chasing a soccer ball, and a sophomore looking for a dress to wear to the spring formal. I remembered every moment in a flash, but I also remembered how I'd allowed grief over Rhia to interfere with my relationship with Lindsay. I remembered the times she'd run up to me to show me something she'd made, but I'd turned away because I was busy with Rhia or I couldn't bear to see the beautiful picture Lindsay had drawn while Rhia was still scribbling.

When the graduation ceremony ended, Lindsay bounced up to me and I hugged her tightly. She hugged me back, then looked at me with shining eyes, saying, "Thank you for being here."

"Of course. I'm so proud of you," I said.

And I meant it. Gone were the envy and negative comparisons between Rhia and Lindsay. Instead, I felt pride in both my girls. For the first time I saw them as the wonderful, unique young women they were. I also saw how much they were like each other. One cousin was able-bodied and one cousin struggled to walk, but both cousins were strong-willed and full of joy. Both girls were unstoppable.

One day during the summer after graduation, I walked into Rhia's room and saw her holding up a book to show her caregiver Rolina's one-year-old son. Rhia pointed to the words and recited them from memory. The baby stared at the pages, completely entranced by the story and Rhia's direction. When Rhia saw me watching, she said, "I'm teaching the baby to read."

"I see," I said. "Can I watch?"

"Okay, but you have to be quiet."

Carefully I sat down on her floor to watch Rhia read to the baby. The baby looked at me one time then returned to focusing on Rhia and the pages of her book.

"This word is 'and.' It starts with an A." Rhia pointed at the word and then moved the book closer to the baby. The baby leaned forward to see what Rhia was pointing at, then reached out his hand and smacked the page. "Be careful," Rhia said. "Books can rip."

Rhia turned a page, held the book up for the baby to see the picture, then recited the words on the page. Again she pointed to a word, this time "the."

When she reached the last page, she said solemnly, "The end." Then she sat the book down. The baby stared at her and at the book. "Do you want me to read more?" Rhia asked. The baby leaned forward and slapped the book with both hands.

Rhia looked at me and said, "I'm a good teacher. The baby wants to learn more."

"You're an excellent teacher," I said, feeling pride in my daughter's eagerness to teach. Then I stood up and left them alone, afraid I would interfere with the lesson.

When Rhia graduated, she said she wanted to be a teacher when she grew up.

She was, in more ways than one.

10

Whenever Rhia heard Stevie Nicks's song "Rhiannon," she would shout, "That's about me!" After she lost her hearing, I told her whenever I heard the song, and she would still grin and proclaim the song was hers. It had been a magical song for me since I heard it as a child and fell in love with Stevie Nicks. In 2013, the song created real magic.

I was at the United Mitochondrial Disease Medical Conference once again, this time in Nashville, Tennessee, and without Rhia. After three days of lectures, research presentations, and keynote speakers discussing living with the disease, I needed a break. I'd been out to the honky-tonks and restaurants with a few people I met at the conference, but that Saturday I decided to go out on my own. It felt good to walk the sidewalks of downtown Nashville alone and without needing to make conversation. I'd had fun with my new friends, but as an introvert I needed some alone time.

Wandering off the honky-tonk–lined main street of downtown Nashville, I heard the unmistakable sound of a blues guitar echoing down a narrow, brick-lined alley. I followed the sound until it led me to a dark but cheerful bar called Bourbon

Street Blues. This felt like the kind of bar where locals came to hear music. The old brick walls were decorated with stickers, bright geometric patterns, and neon signs. Scratched wooden tables with dark brown chairs crowded around a narrow dance floor. There was balcony seating and a long bar close to the front door. On the raised stage was a man playing the guitar music I'd followed and singing classic Memphis blues, my favorite kind of blues. The cheerful, rundown bar and sad blues music fit my melancholy mood. I ordered a gin and tonic with extra lime and listened to his set, finding comfort in music that spoke of hard times since before the Great Depression. When he finished performing, I walked to him and told him how much I loved his music.

"If you like my music, you need to stick around for this band." He waved his hand toward the next group of musicians as they began unloading their instruments. The lead singer was a tall, blond-haired woman in a fringed leather vest who walked over to us. After she hugged the man hello, she held out her hand to me.

"What brings you to Nashville?" she asked.

"I'm here for a medical conference," I said.

"Are you a doctor?"

"No. I'm a parent. My daughter has mitochondrial disease and I came here for the conference to learn more."

The singer and I walked to the bar, where she bought a beer and I bought another gin and tonic. She asked me questions about my daughter and mitochondrial disease, and she seemed so interested I found myself telling her everything: how much Rhia loved to sing even though she was deaf and how hard she struggled to do anything but how much she still laughed and how everyone thought she'd be dead by now . . . plus I was on my third G&T so my usual shyness had vanished.

She asked Rhia's name and I said, "Rhiannon."

"Did you name her after the song?"

I laughed. "Sort of. I named her after the story the song came from."

The drummer crashed his cymbal to get her attention; it was time for the band to start their set. She hopped onto the stage and I found a chair up front. Their music was a mix of blues and classic rock with a twang of Americana mixed in by a fiddler and standing bass.

And then I heard the familiar intro to the song, *Rhiannon.*

"This one's for Terena," the singer said.

When she sang the chorus, every person in the bar joined in.

I laughed and cried and laughed some more, waving my arms in the air every time we sang "Rhiannon" together. There must have been a hundred people in that bar, and every single one was happily singing Rhiannon's name.

This is why Rhia loves to sing, I thought. *Singing is pure happiness.*

When the song ended, I stood and cheered. I think everyone else stood to clap, too. A woman sitting near me asked if I was Terena, and I said yes. Her husband bought me another G&T. We chatted about our children as the band played another song.

All the sadness that had seeped into me from the conference disappeared on that hot July, Nashville night.

Rhiannon. My daughter. The girl I raised and protected. The young woman I am only now beginning to know. I lost her for a while when the fear of losing her overwhelmed me. But I see her now. Strong, funny, kind, and tenacious. Rhiannon . . . Rhia . . . is so much more than a collection of symptoms and disabilities.

She is herself.

Epilogue

As of this writing, Rhia is twenty-eight years old and lives with me. All of the predictions about her death were wrong. We still don't know how long she will live. She has an unidentified type of mitochondrial disease, which means she could live one more year or ten more years. More than likely, Rhia's ataxia will worsen and she'll eventually be unable to walk. But when will that actually happen, and how bad will it get?

I have no idea.

This knowledge isn't easy to live with. There are days I would do anything to have just one clue about Rhia's illness. Just one road map to guide me so I can help her live happily. Instead, I'm left in the dark making up interventions as I go, hoping I'm making the right choices with only one quarter of the information I need. It's a ridiculous way to live your life, but we do it. There isn't an option. I can fall apart on Rhia, or I can keep trying. She refuses to give up, so neither will I.

I still struggle with the balance between helping her medically and harming her emotionally. Nor am I sure when I'm actually supporting her or making choices based on my own ableism. Rhia is conserved because she is unable to make medical decisions for herself, therefore I need to make decisions that protect her health while also considering her own wishes. Since she hates being poked and prodded, I limit all tests to those that are absolutely necessary. There are some tests doctors would like to perform that provide more information and that could lead to more answers about the type of mito she has. Will those tests improve her health or well-being? Probably not, so I follow her wishes and decline the experiments. As much as I long for answers, I can't put her through any more unnecessary medical procedures.

I cannot save her body or cure her illness, but I can protect her mental and emotional health. As long as she keeps singing, I know I'm doing a good job.

A Letter to the Reader

Dear frightened, overwhelmed parent sitting alone in the middle of the night,

> You are not alone.
> There are thousands of us struggling with those
> overwhelming feelings of loss and fear.
> But you can do this. I promise.

On my website are handouts and articles filled with information and guidance, everything from what to do when your child is first diagnosed to how to navigate your first IEP and what happens when your child ages out of school services.

And please email me if you need support or have a question. My contact information is on my website.

We are a community of parents fiercely protecting the children we love and that love is powerful. Remember that.

In solidarity,
Terena
www.terenascott.com

About the Author

Author photo © Tymn Urban

Terena Scott's work is fueled by her passion for art and her belief that everyone, including children with disabilities, has a right to self-expression. She embodies this belief through her work teaching art to children with complex medical needs. A trained teacher of the visually impaired, she also reads stories for visually impaired children on her YouTube channel, "Story Time with Miss Terena." Terena lives and works in the San Francisco Bay Area.

Looking for your next great read?

We can help!

Visit www.shewritespress.com/next-read
or scan the QR code below for a list
of our recommended titles.

She Writes Press is an award-winning
independent publishing company founded to
serve women writers everywhere.

SWP